Proverbs and Sayings
- The Most Famous Ones in the East

by
Akef Soufan

authorHOUSE®

AuthorHouse™ UK Ltd.
500 Avebury Boulevard
Central Milton Keynes, MK9 2BE
www.authorhouse.co.uk
Phone: 08001974150

First published by AuthorHouse 11/9/2007

ISBN: 978-1-4343-4482-3 (e)
ISBN: 978-1-4343-4483-0 (sc)

Printed in the United States of America
Bloomington, Indiana

This book is printed on acid-free paper.

Table of Contents

Preface

The East is the cradle of proverbs, sayings, maxims, wisdoms, tales and fables. The books which treat these subjects are among the most abundant in Eastern literature.

We mention, here, just for the memory, Spiritual Hellenic Wisdom, The Pavilion of Wisdom, books from which drew famous writers and philosophers such as "Aljahiz", Altawhidi", or "Ibn Arabi". All these authors showed the specific importance of this kind of literature which prevailed in eastern civilization.

This collection is less for showing up the wisdoms of Eastern cultures than to be an invitation to a reflection on the universality of human behavior.

We noticed, however, that some sayings and wisdoms are of the nature to influence the individual behavior by canceling all ideas related to innovation or progress within societies deeply marked by the tradition. Our objective, while working to achieve this collection was not to contribute in determining behavior on a moral level, but more, to give the western reader an occasion to think of his own behavior by opening the doorway to the understanding of "the Eastern soul".

This was our objective in collecting these Eastern wisdoms. If the understanding and mutual respect are the basis of all cooperation between people, let's hope that this modest collection will bring, in its way, it's a contribution to this necessary dialogue between cultures at this time of globalization.

The author

Evaluation

Evaluation of the concept of proverbs and sayings in the East.

In the Assyrian-Babylonian language, we find the word "Mathal" (proverb, saying) which signifies "to shine", where as in Arabic, we use "Hukm" (power) and its derivatives such as "Hikma" (wisdom) to evoke power and sovereignty. As for the Hebrew, it kept the word "Mathal" instead of "Hukm" to evoke the power and sovereignty.

The word statue (in Arabic Timthal derived from "Mathal" signifies also in Abyssinian "a thing put in a given form". This statue was in the Semite ancestral spirit, the symbol of sovereignty and hegemony because it was synonymous with protection and continuity by reminding the powerful master from whom we expected good and from whom we feared anger.

Most of researchers agreed that the signification of the word wisdom is more general than that of the proverb. All proverbs or sayings are wisdom whereas all wisdoms are not necessarily proverbs or sayings. We can distinguish the wisdom: a way of acting or thinking which is expressed easily in aphorisms, where the meaning and life experiences are condensed: it is, at least, what we observe in the ancient Greek culture and in the Semitic Culture. *

> Abdel Majid Abdine, Proverbs in ancient Arab Poetry, Beirut, 1971. P 22.

The Semites have used the word "Mathal" (proverb or saying) to indicate "the art of speech". In the Greek language, the proverb is defined as "a brief and famous expression". This Greek definition seems to have reached the East. The Arabs have adopted a similar approach. Ibn Salam considers that the proverb must be concise, with a clear meaning and does a good comparison.

Some thinkers have shown that there was a relationship between proverbs and the old poetry in the Semitic and non Semitic literature and that the old sayings and proverbs taken out from the Sumerian engravings and in the tomes of the Torah belonged to the poetic style of the Semite. The proverb was made up of two equal verses at least. It is worth noting that written proverbs belonged to a register of formal language, a thing which certainly has preserved them from being forgotten.*

> Ibn Abd Rabou – Al Eqd Al Fared - Vol. I11, p63

It is, however, probable from a logical point of view that the oral proverb was born before the beginning of writing for some literary purposes.

Some researchers have remarked the importance of metaphors in the proverbs.

For example, The Babylonians have represented the planets by pictograms.

Researchers have deepened the relationship between the proverb and the metaphor. Some of them even claim that the proverb is the origin of the metaphor.*

Others, in studying the proverbs (or old Semite sayings), have established a relationship between them and power. These researchers think that the proverb, the way it is said, has the word for origin or the speech pronounced by the leader or the master.

> Abdel Majid Abdine, Proverbs in ancient Arab Poetry, Beirut, 1971. P 27.

The proverb would be, thus, the expression of a power practicing control over a given group. That would explain the fact that some expressions attributed to some priests or prophets were recorded in the form of sayings. These men were practicing a religious or secular authority.*

Religions have praised wisdom and have intimately linked it to the Holy Books. The Arabs have recognized the relationship between wisdom and the Book and have named the man who masters the wisdom and the Book by "the verb" or the "perfect". **

➤ Studies of Easterners Concerning the Authenticity of Pre-Islamic Period (Aljahiliya) Beirut House "Dar Al ilm Lilmalayine" House of Science for Millions, 1999.

➤ Soufan Akef – Values of Education in Arab proverbs – Ministry of Education – Abu Dhabi - U.A.E - 1991. p 77.

Popular sayings were not far from the influence of power, some sayings were largely used in the councils and entourage of sovereigns.

Others also came to us in the form of satire, criticism or praise addressed to a person or a group of people in power. After being learned by the sovereigns, the religious men, the sayings were passed on with other knowledge.

If the popular Aramaic or Jewish proverbs have won the reputation that belongs to them, thanks to the interpreters of the Holy Books, and religious men; the Arabs, as for them, before the arrival of Islam, disposed of some cultural centers which largely contributed in propagating numerous sayings, proverbs, tales and wisdoms.*

➤ Soufan Akef – Values of Education in Arab proverbs – Ministry of Education – Abu Dhabi- U.A.E - 1991. p 53

India, undoubtedly, was the cradle of famous tales, proverbs and sayings which were spread all over the world and which were afterward implanted in other regions as China, Tibet, Iran, the Arab World and Old Europe. And from this journey through Indian, Arab Jewish, America, Europe , Far East and Persian sayings, we can notice the similitude and the mutual influence between various eastern and western cultures.

The proverb or saying finds its source sometimes in a story, at other times; it is the beginning of a story it is going to illustrate.

- 1 -
Indian Wisdoms

- 1 -
Indian Wisdoms

The wisdoms and the popular tales remain among the most important folk themes in the Indian civilization constituting the natural and the direct outcome of the beginning of human thought, at the time when mankind was highly attached to symbols and personification.

Indian popular tales have known this evolution throughout human history and have had varied roles.

The tales or fables which make animals speak constitute one of the most important literary forms, either with the general or the level of popular classes or on the level of upper classes of the society.

We can find there the deep roots which brought us back to the pre-philosophical time as we can find symbols which allow one self to express in situations where one could not do otherwise. Indian literature has known some fables episodes which were known for their unequaled literary values such as Kalila & Dimna and the Five Books or Penjatentra*.

➤ La Pajatentra, translation by Dr Abdul hamid Younes, Egyptian General Authority of the Book, Cairo, 1982.

The translation of the Penjatentra cannot but evoke the memory of Kalila & Dimna and can as well compare these two tales to the Eastern wisdom in general such as the Persian and Arab wisdom. This comparison is established by the similarities and differences between cultures.

Researchers can follow the history of tales and wisdoms as one can follow the footprints of a person, and they can notice every evolution related to the difference in the environment and the diversity of cultures through the centuries.

We have also tried to introduce a selection of Indian wisdoms by following as far as possible their sources as samples but not as fixed rules.

Benevolence

1. Do not offer salt or advice to whoever does not request them from you. (Kalila & Dimna, 100 B.C 500AD)*

2. He who loves you for a thing will stop doing so when that thing disappears.

3. Three kinds of persons spoil their good actions: a benefactor who is boastful, the one who does well for someone who does not deserve it and a mother who satisfies an ungrateful son. (Kalila & Dimna). **

➢ Reported otherwise in English Proverbs "Never give advice unasked".

➢ Kalila and Dimna wrote Indian fables which dramatize animals. These were translated in 13th century into ancient Spanish, then to Hebrew by Goel, a religious Jew.

Keeping the secrets

1. Confide your secrets to only one person and ask advice from a thousand others (Taghour).

2. Whoever divulges his secret to someone teaches him to do the same. (Ibn Mukaffa).

3. Never disclose to your friend what you do not wish that your enemy knows. (Ibn Mukaffa).

Friendship:

1. A friend is the opposite of old clothes: the more his friendship is old, the more indefectible it remains. (Ibn Mukaffa). *

2. Three men will not be long to break up: the one who does not help his friend in need, the one who does not visit his friends except in flourishing days, and the one who satisfies himself with good speech. (Kalila & Dimna)**

➢ Reported otherwise by Jim Hayes: "An old friend will help you move, a good friend will help you move a dead body.

➢ Wisdom told otherwise in English Proverbs "Old friends and old wine and old gold are best".

Sadness:

1. Four people will never live without sadness: a rich man who becomes poor, someone who is anxious about his properties, and someone who aspires for a position he does not deserve, and someone who envies others for their prosperity. (Ibn Mukaffa)*

2. Three men feel the sorrow: someone who puts himself in trivial work, someone who breaks off with his friends during their unhappy days and someone who divorces a virtuous woman to get married with an ugly one. (Kalila & Dimna.). **

3. Four men with whom you must not jest: an illustrations and powerful man, a chaste scholar, a vile miser, and a sad man who has lost his child. (Ibn Mukaffa).

➤ Related in another way by Hatem 9th century.

➤ Related in another way by Martin Luther "There is no more lovely, friendly, and charming relationship, communion, or company than a good marriage".

---

4. 5. Three men deserve to be sad: someone who possesses a horse of low productivity, someone preparing much sauce and lastly finds it insipid,

and someone marrying an exemplary woman whose value he is not aware of. (Kalila & Dimna.).*

6. Two men do injustice to themselves: a wealthy man who lives miserably, an old man marrying a young woman who keeps on making fun of him and who can definitely get rid of him. (Kalila & Dimna).

7. A king must not be angry because his power lies in the means in his possession and must neither lie because he would not be compelled to act against his will. (Kalila & Dimna).

8. Five men will never sleep: a rich man who is anxious about his fortune, a poor man laying under the burden of his debt, a sick man without hope for recovery, the one who keeps on envying his neighbors and the one who has committed a crime. (Ibn Mukaffa).

➢ Related in another way in Bible Proverbs "is better to dwell in the corner of the housetop, than with a brawling woman and in a wide house ".

Miscellaneous

1. He who puts himself in a suspicious situation must not blame but himself. (Ibn Mukaffa)*

2. Believe in love, even if it brings you pain. (Taghour**), 1861-1941).

3. The more you get close to modesty the more you reach greatness. (Taghour).

4. Three men will be losers: the one who associates with goldsmith and blacksmith, a trader who marries a young woman and often leaves her for his business trips, and a wise man who associates with traitors and impostors. (Kalila & Dimna). ***

5. Two men must regret their acts: the one who attends a meal to which he is not invited, and the one who asks his friends a favor they cannot render and persists on asking them. (Indian wisdom). ****

➢ Related in another way by Ali Ibn Abi Talib

➢ Taghour : a great poet of the Indian continent - Novel price 1913

➢ Wisdom told otherwise in Bible Proverbs " He that walketh with wise men shall be wise: but a companion of fools shall be destroyed

➢ Reported otherwise in the Abbassed Era.

---

6. 7. Laziness carries along poverty, excess of hesitation causes confusion and suffering. The greedy person never finds rest, even when finding what he wishes. And when he finds it, he doesn't spend it, and for that he accumulates tiredness, avidity and miserliness. (Muawiya, 7th century)

8. Three people are unbearable: a woman who gets married many times and is never satisfied with one husband, a man used to lying and a boastful man. (Kalila & Dimna).

9. Five men lose their virtue: the impudent his praises, the swindler his friends, the impolite his honor, the miser the wealthy life, the lazy the fruits of the work. (Ibn Mukaffa).

10. Four things are helpful for work: health, richness, science, and the divine grace. (Ibn Mukaffa)

11. A rational man must avoid doing enemies by relying on his own force and the one who possesses an antidote should not drink poison by relying on his anti-poison. (Kalila & Dimna).

12. 13. Nothing in this world is living by himself; even the sun is not solitary in its system. Are you more sublime than the Eternal Sun? (Spresh Kohli, Indian poet, the River Speech).

14. It is absolutely against civilization and reason that people kill each other. (Nehru, Great Indian leader born in 1889).

15. I would like to go on long trip carrying water on my chest and have no rest until the world gets rid of its vices. (Abdul Ahad Azad).

16. Youth and wealth vanish rapidly as bubbles in the water. (Penjatentra 100 BC. 500 AD).

17. He who lives in poverty finds it's easy to abandon decency, and the one who abandons decency loses gladness and sense of honor. (Kalila & Dimna).

18. All the forces crumble in front of the tears of a woman. (Taghour).

19. Four things are not long standing: the shade of a coal-miner, the friendship of evil doers, the love of women, and false flatteries. (Kalila & Dimna).

20. 21. When a woman gets angry she breaks the jar containing her secrets.

22. The wooing is the ladder of love and love is its temple.*

➢ Related in another way by James Thurber "Love is what you've been through with somebody".

- 2 -
Persian Wisdom

- 2 -
Persian Wisdom

Introduction to Persian wisdom.

Persian scholars, historians and men of letters were interested in collecting Persian wisdom and proverbs. Among the most important of these

Al Firdawsi, the author of a famous Persian period Shahnami, Farid Eddine Al-Attar, the author of the logic of animals, Djelal Idine Alrumi, Hafez alshirazy, Ibn Sina (Averoes), Omar Al-Khayyam. In the twelfth century of the Gregorian calendar, the latter was highly distinguished from his contemporaries by his closeness to a number of scholars, men of letters and Ulemas in Iran. Letters and arts developed rapidly especially the linguistics sciences, oratorical arts, the wisdoms and proverbs including the divine wisdom. Historians have considered that the period of Omar El-Khayyam was a period of wisdom and considered him as a second Ibn Sina (Averoes) because of his wisdom. His fame owing to his Rubaiyat or quaternary contained some poems of which the wisdom constitutes the lion's share.

In their turn, the Persian wise men, like all eastern wise men, were influenced by the cultural patrimony of other people in particular by what was translated by the Indian wisdom such as Kalila & Dimna and Arabic poetry. If Persian wisdom has adopted what has influenced it throughout eras, it has expressed it in an authentic style.*

If we observe the meticulousness of the style, it would be necessary for the poet or the wise man to paraphrase for himself in order to specify the meaning, because each added word grants inevitably something new to the meaning. Translations went away from the original text because the translator looked after the harmony of the language, in order to keep the hall-mark of that period, with the wish to translate and to present to the reader an original work as if it was not at all a translation.

➢ Soufan Akef – Educative Values of Arab proverbs –Ministry of Education – Abu Dhabi- U.A.E- 1991. p 77.

That was clearly manifested in the poems and the wisdom of Omar Al-Kkhayam. Historians have also demonstrated that he was influenced by Abu Alaa Al Maari.*

He wanted, in fact, to give meaning to such an extent that when referring to the original text we could not find similitude or connection.

He took away from the translation its Arabic cloth and gave it the new spirit of Al-Khayyam, the poet and the wise philosopher.

The pieces of Persian wisdom in prose and in poetry which we present here to the reader express eloquently what we have clearly mentioned.

➢ Waddie Albustani, Rubaiyyat Alkhyiam Beirut, Lebanon 1971.

Sagacity

1. He who does not know the source of evil, would not know how to escape it. (Al Shirazy 12th century)

2. The company of capricious boss and the fact of trying to satisfy nasty people are the most distressing things. (Al Shirazy)

3. The magnanimous soul is the one that misfortunes do not affect and a dignified soul is the one that does not feel the weight of burdens. (Al Shirazy).

4. What makes the women respectful with their husbands: satisfaction, chastity, harmonious coexistence, lack of reproaches and jealousy. (Al Shirazy)

Reason

1. We asked a wise man: "What are the fruits of reason?", he replied: "Do not be delighted at praise if you do not deserve it, do not hate the one who objectively criticizes you and don't do anything that you will regret afterwards. (Al Shirazy).

2. Do not dispute with your brothers even if you are eloquent. (Ibn Salam, 8th century)*

3. If you do not think of all you loose all. (Ibn Salam).

4. If you want to be obeyed, give orders that could be carried out. (Ibn Salam)**

➢   Related in another way In Kalila & Dimna.

➢   Related in another way by Aljahiz & Ali Bin Abi Talib.

Destitution and richness

1. Know that the source of poverty is wastefulness, the source of richness is good planning, and that of praise is generosity, the source of humiliation is begging

2. Your share in possessions is what belongs to you. Your dignity through your ethics is eternal. Whereas money disappears with time, morals and virtues never grow old. (Al Shirazy).

3. Oh, friend, spend if you gather richness, and do not endure the agonies to conserve them. The bird of time stays for a moment, and then it flies and never comes back again. (Omar Alkayam).

4. You have for possession only your limited days: the elapsed days will never come again. (From the Abbasid Era)

5. A wise man must not rejoice of enormous wealth, and must not become sad in famine time. He who is considered truly rich is the one who shares his fortune with others, and a real benefit is what we get without praises. (One of the kings in Persian Empire).

Miscellaneous

1. What causes more shame to one's fellow is the weakness of a leader, the wrath of scholars, obscenity of women, the sickness of doctors, the lies of judges. (Al Shirazy).

2. Three things have unpleasing consequences: an ill-tempered man, a passion stirred up with short-lived pleasures and carelessness in the work.*

3. The best quality of kings lies in their dignity at the moment of anger, the leniency and serenity they show. Their worst defects are: virulence, lack of patience and intelligence, and their negligence of the general interest. (Ibn Salam).

➢ Wisdom told other wise in French Proverbs " Work relieves us from three great evils, boredom, vice, and want"

➢ Differently related in English Proverbs "A stitch in time saves nine".

---

4. 5. The ancient Persians did not entrust the borders control except to a person combining eleven qualities peculiar to animals:

    To be as a quick as a horse.
    To have the eyes of a lynx.

To know well one's way as the grouse.
To be as audacious as a lion.
To jump as well as a cheetah.
To be as cunning as a fox.
To be as arrogant as a jackal.
To be as fearless as a panther.
To be as thrifty as an ant.
To guard as well as a dog.
To be as abstentious as a donkey.
(Of the Abbassid Era, Al Jahiz).

6. Avoid cowardice, otherwise you will be despised. Breaking with one's friends brings regret.

7. Know also that the source of salvation is probity, the source of greatness is nobility, and know that hatred and enmity can come from a tasteless joke or of being too outspoken." (Of the Abbassid Era, Al Jahiz 9th –12th century).*

➢ Wisdom told other wise in Spanish Proverbs"
A word from the mouth is like a stone from a sling".

---

8. 9. Virtue can be acquired only by a continued struggle against egocentrism and passion. A vice is enough to erase many virtues. And know that virtue exists in every social environment, every

race of human kind and cannot be sold at any price. (Alshirazy)*

10. Know that benefits are numerous: good health, tranquility of soul and body are better than the whole earth. Avoid envying others because you may enjoy a godsend they are lacking. Try hard to show gratitude of the kind deeds you are filled with. (Ibn Salam).

11. Nothing is more harmful to an old man than a young beautiful girl and a good cook. (Averoes, 980-1037).

12. What makes love unique is that with the suffering it engenders, it may give birth to happiness. (Averoes, 980-1037).

➤ Old otherwise in American Proverbs:" Ask questions from you heart and you will be answered from the heart".

---

13. 14. I have solved all the problems, I have avoided all the traps and ambushes, and I have untied all ties except that of death. (Omar Alkiyam)

15. The vigilance of a judge is better than two irreproachable witnesses. (Almaidany, 11th century).

16. One can bring his horse to the water, but cannot compel him to drink. (Hakki).*

17. If I let a word go, it becomes my master. (Persian king).

> ➤ Related in English Proverbs.

---

18. 19. I have encountered in life only tiredness and misfortune. What a pity! If my day has come and my spirit would not manage to decipher the mystery of destiny. (Omar Alkiyam)*

20. The one you associate with in life and to whom you are close might be in reality an enemy. (Omar Alkayam).

21. We fear many things that do not happen; we often make more worries than what is there in reality.

22. Be like the sandalwood, it perfumes the axe which cuts it. (Al Shirazy).

23. You would better walk bare feet than with very narrow shoes. (Al Shirazy).

24. Do not expose yourself to sun rays and avoid the infernal heat of the midday. (Averoes).

25. A beautiful face creates passion, whereas a nice voice nourishes the soul. (Al Shirazy).

> ➤ Differently related by Martin Luther King "If a man hasn't discovered something that he will die for, he isn't fit to live".

- 3 -
Arab Wisdom

- 3 -
Arab Wisdom

Introduction

Specialists in Arabic language, especially men of letters, poets and historians were interested in collecting wisdom and proverbs. They have worked to explain and to study them. In this perspective, we have "majmaa al-amthal" (the collection of proverbs) by Al Meidani, kitab al-amthal by Al Bagdady, "Al torfa Al bahiya" by Hamza Al Isfahany and the collection of proverbs only to mention a few In the beauty of wisdom, we find Adab Al dine wal Dunia by Alhassan Al Bassry (morality of life and religion), the works of Abuhayan Tewhidy ,particularly the book of amtal wa mu'anassa (proverbs and conviviality) and the works of Aljahiz of which the most important are: albyan wa al tebyeen (rhetoric and eloquence),kitab alhaywan (the book of Animals) and so on.

The wisdoms were the kind of speech most wide spread in the Arabic language mainly in the everyday speech where the need of these wisdoms was more important than the need of wisdom in other parts of speech.

The user is not obliged to know the author of the wisdom. What matters is its impact and origin in order to portray it and place it in its appropriate context.

Much Arab wisdom was quoted before and after Islam without referring to a known author. This has driven some contemporary researchers to say that it is impossible to distinguish between the Arab wisdom before and after Islam and between the "new born ones".*

The aims of wisdoms and proverbs of the Arabs were intimately linked although they are different in origin and style. The proverb becomes a kind of wisdom when the wisdom marks it with a seal of abstraction, and wisdom becomes a proverb when it achieves one condition: diffusion and popularization.

➤ Jassim Al Abdulla collection of popular Proverbs.

➤ Al Bahrain House of Edition and diffusion, 1984. P 20.

Experiences

1. Don't consult a very busy man even if he is very wise, neither a coward even if he is the most learned. (Ali Ibn Abi Talib)*.

2. Never quarrel with a judge, he will always find a means to beat you. (Ibn Abbass, 7th century).

3. Conjugal relations take four forms: passion, pleasure, recovery and remedy. (Bada'u Zuhur: The marvels of flowers).

4. We are richer than peasants but they are nobler than us. (Jebran Khalil Jebran)**

5. Eat what you like but dress up the way people like. (Ali Bin Abi Talib 7TH C.)

6. Try to forget the mistakes of your friends if you want their friendship to last. (Bashar Ibn Burd, 8th century).

7. The one who tests different situations knows the essence of mankind. (Ali Bin Abi Talib 7th)

➢ Ali cousin of prophet Muhamed the fourth kalifa born in Mecca died in 661AD

➢ Jebran: poet and man of letters, born in 1883. He emigrated to the USA and studied les beaux arts in Paris

---

8. 9. The best meal is the one served the soonest. (Alhajaj)*.

10. Know that your opinion cannot be applied to all. So, keep it for the most important. Your money cannot be enough for everything. So, give more interest for good deeds **

11. Don't stay too long in the "souks," and if you can avoid them it would be much better, for the "souks" are the dustbins of cities. (Ali Ibn Abi Talib).

12. Don't let envious people know your wealth, don't come across to drunkards and don't engage a debate with eloquent people. (Ibn Abass).

13. I have never known a political man who does not lie, a military man who doesn't brag, a newly rich man who doesn't waste money, and a person who has achieved a good deal behaving correctly. (Mustapha AL Sibai). ***

14. Remember that life is full of joys and happiness, far more than some problems we encounter everyday. (Soufan, A)

➤ Al Hajaj ibn Youssouf Al Thakafi Oumeyad commander who ruled Iraq.

➤ Differently related by Hassan Ibn Saida

➢ Mustapha AL Sibai : Egyptian contemporary man of letters .

---

15. 16. Things in this world are easy and difficult at the same time, and you would never reach an easy situation unless you encounter hindrances. If you find yourself in a situation where ease predominates, be aware of the pleasure you get and of the difficulties that this situation contains. (9th century).

17. Don't ask the hungry anything until he satisfies his hunger, nor the thirsty until he satisfies his thirst. (Al-Ahnaf Ibn Qais, 6th -7th century)*

18. The love path ends when the ownership path begins. **

19. Eloquence is speaking without mistakes, and that you hasten and not slow down. (Sahari Alabdi)

20. If you want to know where someone got his money, look where he spent it. (Hassan Ibn Ali, 7th century).

21. The best speech is the one where the meaning is funny; the structure is noble and soft to the ears of its hearers. (Kaab Ibn Safwan). ***

➢ Wisdom told otherwise In American Proverbs "
A hungry stomach makes a short prayer Paiute

> ➤ Differently related in German Proverbs" A hungry man has no conscience".

> ➤ Wisdom told otherwise in Bible Proverbs "A word fitly spoken is like apples of gold in pictures of silver".

---

22. 23. Three are difficult to bear: being compelled to leave a loved land, leaving friends and losing a beloved one. (Zuheir Ibn Abi Salma).

Women

1. Man imagines happiness, but it is woman who leads him to it. (Qassim Amin)*

2. If you are worried by the vices of your wife, remember her virtues, because it is rare that a woman lacks virtue. (Told otherwise in Kalila and Dimna).

3. The woman who chased Adam from paradise by malice made me happy by her love and her affection. (Jebran Khalil Jebran)**

4. The politeness of a woman towards her husband: to show piety during his absence, satisfaction with what he offers her always is smiling, and generous with his relatives. (Arab wisdom told partially in Kalila & Dimna). ***

5. With a compassionate woman life is a paradise; with a dissatisfied one life is a hell. (Anis Mansour)****

➤ Kassim Amin : Egyptian man of letters who defended the women rights

➤ Told otherwise in American Proverbs" A good wife is the best household furniture".

➤ Differently related by Jaime Young "The most precious possession that ever comes to a man in this world is a woman's heart."

> ➤ Related in another way in Bible Proverbs "is better to dwell in the corner of the housetop, than with a brawling woman and in a wide house ".

---

6. The perfect political man is the one who succeeds in politicizing his wife. (Hakki Haroun).

7. A woman can get the secret out of a man's heart whereas it is difficult for a man to discover the secret concealed by his wife. (Anis Mansour)

8. Women listen to the advice of every man except their husband. (Hakki Haroun).

9. Women understand everything except their husband.

10. The woman's reason lies in her beauty whereas the beauty of man lies in his reason. (Elias Qounsoul, 20th century).

11. Do not believe in a woman when she swears, but believe in her when she reddens. (Hakki Haroun).

12. Do not ask your husband to explain his behaviors - where he was and with whom - so not to blame him in case he lies. (Anwar Wajdi).

13. The woman weeps before her marriage and a man weeps after it. (Elias Qounsoul).*

> ➤ Syrian poet and man of letters who lived in Brazil. He belonged to the writers of Exile, born in Yabroud, near Demascus.

---

14. A woman who loves her husband likes to see him constantly happy. (Elias Qounsoul).

15. The shanty where a woman laughs is better than a palace where she weeps. (Jebran Khalil Jebran).

16. It is impossible to live with or without women. (Anis Mansour)

17. Whatever is our attachment to women, sometimes we feel happy in their absence. (Sanabilu Zaman, Ears of time).

18. Man holds dear the woman twice: the day he marries her and the day of her death. (Bada'u Zuhur, the Marvels of flowers)

19. Do not let a stupid woman breast-feed your children because she will affect their character. (Ali Ibn Abi Taleb).

20. Womankind softens the lifestyle and weakens morality. (Al-Nidham, 9th century)

21. We never ask how old an authentic piece of art is, nor how old is a woman. (Sanabilu, Zaman, Ears of time).

22. Four things reduce sadness: the words of a woman, the meeting of friends, a drink taken with smile and good wishes to cheer up your days. (Al-Nidham 9th century)

23. The best companion in times of weakness is a faithful woman, in times of fear reason, and at the moment of death praises. (Muawiya, 7th century)*

24. Marriage is like a meal cooked by vapor: it is healthy but tasteless. (Anis Mansour)

25. The one who submits to his passions remains deprived of his forces, the one who is a slave to his stomach and to concupiscence remains without honor and will never is a honest man. (Al Mamun, 9th century)**.

26. The contemplation of God in women is the noblest, the most perfect, and the most sublime achievement of this contemplation is the act of love. (Ibn Arabi).

➤ Differently related in English Proverb: "All good things must come to an end.

➤ Al Mamun Ibn Haroun Rashid, Abbasid caliph (813-830 AD).

---

27. 28.   A valuable woman will always stands by her husband, enjoys what he enjoys, even if she find difficulties in doing so, and is saddened by what saddens him. She behaves like a sister who respects her elder brother. She is satisfied with

what he offers her, be it little, and limits criticism in his behavior. (Al-Nidham, 9th century)

29. The mother is like a school that, well-formed, can form an exemplary nation. (Ahmed Shawqi, 19th 20th century)

30. Paradise is under mothers' feet (prophet Mohamed 7th century).

Bad Speech

1. The one who tells people what they do not like, people will tell of him what they do not know. (Ali Ibn Abi Talib-7th century)

2. Everything has a beginning and the beginning of enmity is teasing. (Al-Mamun, 9th century)

3. The one who spreads what people say makes his neighbor suspicious and arouses the hatred of other people. (Ibn Abass, 7th century)*

4. The Sultan and women flee someone who solicits with brutality. (Abdul Malik Ibn Marmwan, 7th - 8th century) **

5. Four types of person demean themselves: A talkative man when we do not ask him to speak and says what he does not know, a tyrannical man, a bad servant who denies the saying of his master, and the one who gets in without permission. (Al Mansour Abu Ja'far 8th) ***

> ➢ Ibn Abbass, Abdullah, companion of the prophet Muhammad, known of his recital of hadiths (Prophet's tradition).

> ➢ Ibn Marwan, one of the Umayyad caliphs, the most known for his wisdom and knowledge. He reigned in Damascus in 685 - Related in another

way in Bible Proverbs "Withdraw thy foot from thy neighbour's house; lest he be weary of thee and so hate thee ".

➢ Al Mansur; second Abbasid caliph, he built Baghdad and was interested in science and literature

6. 7. Do not insult your neighbor, do not chase a poor man begging for charity: if he is worthy of your help, does it, if he is deleterious, you would not have given him the occasion to tell bad things about you. (Ibn Abass).

8. Do not jest with a noble, because he might hate you, nor with a vile man because he might harm you. (Saad Ibn Abi Waqass 7th Century).

Hypocrisy and Lowerness

1. Borrowed jewelry: to wear it is a scandalous richness; to give it back is a humiliation. (Al-Hassan Bin Ali 7th Century)

2. Some characteristics of vileness: tendency to fall again in vice after having reached perfection, characteristics of vileness: imitate the weak people when one is at the paroxysm of his forces. (Ali Ibn Abi Talib)

3. Be careful to someone who praises you when you do not deserve it: He might ignore a good thing you did to him. (Ali Ibn Abi Talib)

4. We asked a wise man: "Which is the most dangerous for a man: pretentiousness or hypocrisy? He replied: "Pretentiousness is more dangerous for yourself and hypocrisy for others who come across you, because they are not bewaring your apparent serenity, while you can deceive them at any moment". (Maaruf Al Karkhi).

Arts and Beauty

1. Art is an oasis where man rests from the tiredness of life. (Jebran Khalil Jebran)

2. An ignorant doctor can kill one person whereas a mediocre artist can kill a whole nation. (Jebran Khalil Jebran).

3. The artist is a foreigner among his neighbors and friends, a foreigner in his native land; he is even a foreigner in this world. (Jebran Khalil Jebran).

4. Who would sell me a good thought for loadings of gold? Who would like a handful of pearls for a minute of love? Who would give me an eye which contemplates beauty and take all my treasures? (Jebran Khalil Jebran).*

5. My soul, you are going up to your end. Be patient. Does not hurry up until the flowers grow on my tomb? (Jebran Khalil Jebran)*

6. The Arabs say: Beauty is imbedded in the nose, the charm in the eyes, and the gentleness in the mouth. (Al-Ahnaf Ibn Qais, 7th century).

➤ Differently related in english wisdoms" Anger and hate hinder good counsel".

> ➤ Related in another way in American proverbs "They are not dead who live in the hearts they leave behind".

___

7. We asked a philosopher about beauty. He replied:

- "Of music: strings between the fingers of a woman, horns in the mouth of men;

- Of bird: the eagle because he tries to reach the stars,

- Of nature: mountains, because they elevate looks and ideas,

- Of sea: its calm in the day, its swells in the night;

- Of season: the morning of summer, the midday of spring, the evening of winter, and the night of autumn.

- Of water: its flow because it is like a heart which never knows hatred.

- Of tears: those of a virgin, because they are pure and those of a hero because they are proud;

- Of the sun: its rise because it is a serenity with a smile, and its setting because it is a farewell with hope;

- Of beneficence: charity, because like the rain it arrives in due time. (Al-Jahiz, of the Abbasid Era 9-12th Century).

8. 9. Art is a means of communication with humanity. (Jebran Khalil Jebran)

10. Love in the heart of the one who feels it is more sublime than in the eye of one who sees it. (Ibn Alfared, 8th century)*

11. The beauty of arts constitutes the beauty of a nation. (Jebran Khalil Jebran).

12. I have recited the Indian wisdom, poetry of the Arabic peninsula and the western music. Yet, I am still blind and deaf. (Jebran Khalil Jebran).

13. A nice calligraphy, for the Emir, is perfection, for the rich man a beauty, for the poor a source of income. (Ali Ibn Abi Talib).

14. Each art has its secret. The individual must go beyond accessible reality to reach the world of art. The fear of criticism remains an obstacle to creativity and progress. (Soufan. A)

➤ Differently related in french proverb "Baeauty, unaccompanied by virtue, is as a flower without perfume".

Love and nobility

1. A lover finds the sky clear despite the number of clouds covering it.(Qassim Amin, 20th century).

2. Your love for a thing is a barrier between yourself and its disadvantages. Your disdain for a thing is a barrier between yourself and its advantages. (prophet Mohamed 7th century,)*

3. When a woman roars of anger, four kisses are enough to calm her. (Speech related to love and woman).

4. When love is authentic, it doesn't diminish after marriage. (speech related to love and woman)

5. It seems that here-below, life hears our voices, so it turns its back on those who curse it and embraces those who love it. The love of others opens the door to luck and shut the door to failure and bad luck (Jebran Khalil Jebran).

> ➤ The prophet Mohamed bin Abdullah, prophet pf Islam was born in Mekka in 571 and die in Meddina 632.

---

6. 7. Love is that fruitful feeling which enables us to live fully our nice days and to weave this same joy for others. (Nizar Qabbani, 20th century).*

8. If you think you are worthier than others are, go and teach them. If you acknowledge that they are worthier than you are, socialize with them to learn from them. (Abu Ja'far Al Mansur, 8th century).

9. Wealth kills someone without pain whereas love makes him live even with pain. (Ibn Salam, 8th century)**

10. Our words about love kill it; the letters lose their meaning and die once pronounced. Love is not an eastern tale, at the end of which heroes get married. (Nizar Qabbani)***.

11. I would rather go to the sea without vessel, and have the feeling that it is impossible to reach the harbour. (Nizar Qabbani).

➤ Differently related by Robert A. Heinlein "Love is the condition in which the happiness of another person is essential to your own".

➤ Ibn Salam, a man of letters, the most famous of the Abbasid era. Among his master pieces , the classes of poets.

➤ Syrian poet, one of the most famous contemporary poets mainly in erotic poetry.

---

12. Your figure stands in front of my eye, and your last dwelling is in my heart. (Nizar Qabbani).

13. When you meet them during their sessions, you look like a light breeze, and they look like tree leaves. (Nizar Qabbani).

14. If you expect people to love you, be the first to love them. (Ali Ibn Abi Talib)*

15. Love your dear one within limits; for fear that, he might hate you some day. (Ali Bin Abi Talib)**

16. If you love, do it without excess, and if you hate. ***

17. Do not look at the one who speaks, but at what he says. (Hatim Al Taii)****

➤ Differently related by Plato "At the touch of love, everyone becomes a poet".

➤ Related in another way in English proverbs "The greatest hate springs from the greatest love".

➤ Differently related by Bertrand Russell "Of all forms of caution, caution in love is perhaps the most fatal to true happiness".

➤ Hatim : one of the most famous wise men in the Jahiliya era (before Islam), known for his legendary generosity

---

18. 19. Tears flowing from the lover's eyes are like the most precious pearl in the ring of the most beautiful woman in the world. (Nizar Qabbani.).

20. The end of love is ownership and the end of ownership is destruction.

21. A beautiful woman does not have friends, but lovers and envious women (Salem Aljasser, 20th century).

22. The most successful man for a woman is the most deceitful and most proud.

Timidity

1. Avoid doing bad deeds when alone or with others. Be ashamed of yourself more than any one else. Get used to moderation, both in your deeds and in your speech. (Abul Malik Ibn Marwan).

2. Do not be ashamed of three things: knowledge, sickness, and a poor relative. (Al Mamun, 9th century).

3. The greatest politeness is to be ashamed of oneself. (Ali Bin Abi Talib 7th)

Cupidity, miserliness, generosity

1. Whoever deprives himself is accumulating for others. (Ali Bin Abi Talib 7th century)

2. Money is like love. It kills the miser and brings the life to the one who gives it. (Al-Ahnaf Ibn Qais, 6th century).*

3. Never think that a stingy man can be honest .There is never honesty with miserliness. (Omar Ibn Abdelaziz 7 -8th century).

4. We asked a wise man: "Who are the kings?" he replied: "The chaste ones". We asked him "and the vile ones?" he replied: "Those who live on the religion's trade". (Omar Ibn Abdelaziz).

5. Generosity makes one close to his enemies, whereas cupidity makes one far from his own sons. (Ali Bin Abi Talib)**

6. A stingy man naively invites his wife to adore every generous man. (Rawdatu alward: The garden of roses).

➢ Differently related by Francis Bacon "Money is like muck, not good except it be spread".

➢ Differently related by Jim Rohn "Giving is better than receiving because giving starts the receiving process".

---

7. Imam Zein Al Abidine used to kiss the hands of the poor men every time he offers charity. We asked him "Why?" he replied that charity falls in the hand of God before falling in the hand of the poor. (Omar Ibn Abdelaziz)*.

8. Do not pick all the fruits leave some for the passers-by. (Prophet Muhammad). **

9. The one who puts on the clothes of generosity is hiding his vices from the eyes of the people. (Prophet Muhammad).

10. The possessions of a stingy person will be destroyed either by accident or by inheritance. (Prophet Muhammad).

11. "Cupidity: someone claims what he is not entitled for, whereas miserliness is refusing to return their rights to his fellows. Cupidity is the most dangerous because it is the origin of evil, and the tool of oppression. The needs of a greedy person never have limits". We asked him "What is the best virtue?" he replied "Reason and knowledge." (From the Abbasid era 9th -12th centuries Al-Jahiz).

➢ Fifth caliph known for his justice and wisdom

➢ Differently related by Arapaho "Take only what you need and leave the land as you found it".

---

12. Three things spoil the good character: cupidity, miserliness and anger. (Ali Bin Abi Talib 7th).

13. Miserliness includes all bad behavior. The generous becomes a master and the miser becomes vile. (Al-Hassan Ibn Ali).

14. You see a miser gathering a lot for his inheritance, and he protects his field like a hungry hunting, keeping its prey for others.*

15. Poverty is a greedy soul, a strong despair, and he who deprives himself gathers for the others. (Al Mawardi).

16. People who offer engender love to the soul and dress it with beauty. (Al Mutanabi). **

➢ Related in another way in German proverbs " The last shirt has no pockets.(Piling up money won't serve you anything once you're dead)

➢ Wisdom told other wise in Bible proverbs " Ointment and perfume rejoice the heart: so doth the sweetness of a man's friend by hearty counsel".

Asking in case of need

1. Nothing is uglier than submission in case of need and pride in case of richness. (Ali Bin Abi Talib)*

2. To be deprived of what ones need is better than asking for it to those who do not possess it. (Muawiya).

3. If you ask something to a magnanimous person, give him the time to think, because he thinks only of good. In addition, if you ask an ill-omened person, hurry him on, because if he thinks a lot, he comes back quickly to his nature. (Ali Bin Abi Talib)

➤ Reported other wise in Spanish proverbs "It's more blessed to give than to receive".

---

4. 5. He who intercedes on behalf of someone and accepts a gift he offers him has committed a great sin. (prophet Muhammad)*.

6. We asked a wise man: "What is the bitterest thing?" He said, "To be in need of people who are not worth of being asked". (from the Abbasid era 9th-12th centuries Al-Jahiz)

7. The one who doesn't ask others gains their respect. (Ibin Al Arabi)

8. The heritance of a defunct is a pride for his heirs.

9. The abstentious person is easily met by friends and the needy one has a boring face. (Al Mutanabi).

> ➤ Differently related in English proverbs" Who receives a gift, sells his liberty".

Anxiety and sadness

1. Be fond of sane things: a sweet smell strengthens the good thinking and the cleanliness of clothes diminishes worries (Abdul Malik Ibn Marwan).*

2. Be dignified and do not claim to get what you cannot reach. Avoid having two faces or two speeches and do not backbite absent people. (Abassid era, Jahiz, 9th –12th century)

3. The two saddest persons are those who sleep while working and those who work while sleeping (sanabil al zaman, ears of time).

➤ Differently related in Holy Bibl proverbs, "Ointment and perfumes rejoice the heart".

Bliss

1. the most pleasant: "exchanging jokes with those we like, conversing with honest people, and expressing good wishes to strengthen our hopes in the future. (bu Nawass- Al Hassan Ibn Hani'i)*

2. Happiness is to deeply understand that you will never make others happy; unless happiness shines on your face and that you give up materialistic possessions which get you away from spiritual richness and serenity. (Al Ahnaf Ibn Qais). **

3. The most comforting thing is security, and the happiest life is that of a person who lives among wise people. (Ali Bin Abi Taleb).

➢ Abu Nawass Hassan Ibn Hani'I, born in 756 in South Iran, died in 815 in Baghdad, one of the most famous poets of the Abbasid era.

➢ Differently related by Baltasar Gracian"Friendship multiplies the good of life and divides the evil".

---

4. I have not suffered from anxiety by living in the desert, there, in paradise; I have found tranquility and satisfaction. (Jebran Khalil Jebran).

5. If your wife and children do not offer you calm and happiness, try to get leisure, otherwise you

shall spend your life in horror. (Aktham Bin saifi, 6th century)*

6. You will never know how to be happy until you have understood that life is worth more if it is spent far from materialism. (Jebran Khalil Jebran).

7. Happiness relies on four things: good behavior, common sense, abundance of assets and love from others. (Abbassid era 9-12th C, Jahiz).

➢ The wise of the Arabs before Islam.

➢ Differently related by Honore de Balzac "One should believe in marriage as in the immortality of the soul".

➢ Wisdom told otherwise, by Dan Wilcox "I don't care how poor a man is; if he has family, he's rich".

---

8. 9. We say: "If the servant is happy in his relationship with his master, his life on earth will be similar to his life in the hereafter, that his death is similar to his life, his indigence similar to his richness, his sickness similar to his health, his weakness similar to his force, his sadness similar to his joy. (Al Jahiz).

10. With three things, we are never alone: good behavior, abstention from evil and the fact of

avoiding bad suspicions. (Sanabilu al zman, ears of time).

11. Happiness is not having every thing, but having what we need. (Said Akel)

Travel and Exile

1. If you find yourself in a country other than yours, forget about what you know and adapt your mind to that of the natives and try to remain humble. (Sanabilu al zman, ears of time).

2. Happiness is the satisfaction in one's home country. (Ibn Alarabi, 8th century).

3. Four elements contribute to man's happiness: a compassionate wife, an obedient child, a faithful friend and living in one's own country. (Omr Ibn Ahtam, 5-6th centuries)

4. Knowledge is a homeland for exiles, whereas ignorance is an exile in one's own country. (Ali Bin Abi Talib)

Smiling faces

1. Good luck is like a guest, it escapes when it discovers a grumpy face. (Abu Ja'far El Mansur -712-775)*

2. Do not blame good luck when it refuses to come close to dark faces and if it visits smiling ones. (Ibn Safwan, 8th century, nuzahatu alhikma)**

3. Of the politeness of a man towards his wife: to be a pleasant companion, to have good speech, to show beneficence towards her relatives, to keep his promises, to avoid fruitless discussions and jealousy and never quarrel with her. (Al Jahiz, 10th century) ***

4. Four things strengthen love: joy, good deeds, will for harmony, and absence of differences. (Ali Ibn Abi Taleb).

➤ Wisdom told otherwise, in English proverb "We must live by the living, not by the dead".

➤ Ibn Sawan Khald, one of the most eloquent Arabs in the Umayyad era.

➤ Al Jahiz, one of the most famous men of letters in the Abbasid era.

---

5. Smiling to an ugly person shows beneficence and it is much better than marveling in front of beauty. (Al Qarawi, 19th-20th centuries)*.

6. Face is the index of the heart (Zuheir Bin Abi Salma).

7. Don't be angry, for you will not be able to judge things accurately, and you would say words or commit deeds, which you may regret and will be accountable for. (Omr ibn Al Ass)

8. Don't be gloomy during your work, a smile doesn't cost you anything, and its effect is great on those you are dealing with, and never interfere in the work of others.

➢ Lebanese poet and man of letters

➢ Reported otherwise in Japanese proverbs" The eye is the mirror of the heart".

Veneration and Faith

1. If prayer is an aspect of obedience to the creator, work, as well, is a form of veneration when accompanied by good will (Al Mamoun).

2. He who doesn't see the kingdom of Heaven here and now, will not see it in the hereafter, even if he is a good believer. (Jebran Khalil Jebran).

3. Death is easy for the one who has the conviction of the hereafter and is difficult for the one who doubts it. (AbuJavar Almansur).

4. This universe is run by a force full of wisdom and intelligence, that our simple mental faculties are unable to perceive. (Jebran Khalil Jebran).

Luck and Wealth

1. If people respect you for your money or your authority, don't believe it, because respect goes with the disappearance of its cause. (Ali Ibn Moussa).

2. Don't worry about what is no longer recoverable, because you will never catch the machine of time again. (Jebran Khalil Jebran).

3. Neither seeks recovery by a simple wish, nor security without paying its price. (Arab wisdom of Indian origin, Ibn Muquaffaa, 724-759)*

➢ Wisdom told otherwise In American Proverbs: "There are three kinds of people; those that make things happen, those that watch things happen and those who don't know what's happening".

---

4. No one is beyond an accusation we address him, or a suspicion we inflict on him. For that, appeal to reason; try as far as you can to give back their rights to those deprived of them. (From the Abbasid Era)

5. Only we can engender good or bad luck. (Abbass Mahmoud El Aqad, 20th century). *

➢ Wisdom told otherwise, in Latin proverbs "It is stupid to complain about misfortune that is your own fault & in French Proverbs" fortune helps him that's willing to help himself".

Reason

1. Three things destroy reason: To linger over looking at women, laughing too much, and the contemplation of stars. (Sanabilu al zman, ears of time).

2. Be rational, and you will win tranquility of the soul, rest for the heart, calm for the nerves and happiness of life. (Al-Hassan Ibn Ali, 7th Century).

3. Be moderate and walk aside. (Ibn Salam, 8th C.)

4. The one, who knows the way people think, can avoid their hot temper. (From the Abbassid era).

5. The weakness of man appears when a woman starts wooing him. (Speech related to love and women).

6. Keep close to wise men, friends or enemies are they, because living together with intelligence is fruitful. (Oumar Ibn Abdalaziz, 8th C.)*

7. Youth, idleness and money destroy reason. (Abu Al Atahiya)**

➤ Wisdom told other wise in American proverbs "If we wonder often, the gift of knowledge will come".

➤ Told in another way in American proverbs" Cherish youth, but trust old age".

---

8. 9. A charitable man feels pain if he only works for himself and a wise man feels tired if he talks to a silly man. (Ibn Abass 7th C.).

10. The one who has a soft speech makes many friends. (Alqarawi).

11. Reason provokes good luck, distracts in solitude, drives out poverty, makes the fortune fruitful and allows one to make many friends. (From the Abbasid Era, 9-12th C, Aljahiz).

12. If reason controls passion, it transforms vices into virtues. The happy man is the one whose best fortune is knowledge. (Ibn Dureid 8th C.)

13. Power does not make strong the one who lacks reason, money does not make rich the one who is never satisfied. (Ibn Dureid 8th C.)*

14. When reason becomes perfect, speech diminishes. (Ali Bin Abi Talib)

15. The gift is the proof of the intelligence of the one who offers it. (Abd Almalik ibn Marwan).

➢ Wisdom told other wise in Kelila and Dimna.

Patience

1. Men make as much noise as a tempest, and I can breathe quietly because I find that the violence of the tempest becomes blurred. The calm remains as long as God is there. (Jebran Khalil Jebran).

2. A soft fire allows the preparation of a good meal (Nezhatu al fittna-consequences of the sagacity).

3. The love of a thing makes one blind and deaf. (Prophet Muhammad).

4. Do not take medicine except in case of necessity for it does not cure an ache without causing another. (nezhatu al fittna, (consequences of the sagacity)

5. When a problem appears, it is just one; if you are affected by this fact, you are creating two. (Ali Ibn Abi Talib).

6. 7. Four characteristics of ignorance: an unjustified anger, ignoring oneself, a meaningless speech, and respect for those who do not deserve it. (Ali Ibn Abi Talib).

8. Whoever does not sadden for what he did will gain rest. (Akthem Ibn Saifi, 6th C).

9. If you hear many comments around you, good or bad, be patient, do not try to avoid hearing them.

If you hear a lie make sure to be patient and let no one lead you to a hateful action, think well before acting so that others do not criticize your acts. (from the abbassi era 9-12th C., Aljahiz)

10. Don't feel unlucky, because you were not born at the expense of anyone else. Be yourself, no one looks like you and that is a great fortune. (Ahnaf Ibn Qaiss, 7th C.) **

➤ Told otherwise in American proverbs" Quarreling is the weapon of the way".

➤ Wisdom told other wise by John Stuart Mill" Ask yourself whether you are happy and you seas to be so".

Time

1. Do not evaluate time by saying "It was yesterday, and it will be tomorrow" because there is, in the present hour all time with all its pleasant and achievable hopes. (Jebran Khalil Jebran).

2. Three elements are proofed when a man becomes rich and improves his conditions: his former servant, his first wife and his old house which he is going to destroy to build a new one. (Al Eshaabi)*

3. Never sleep before writing your will even if you are in good health because you do not know what life is hiding for you. (Al Mamun).

➤ Al Shaabi: Judge in the Umayyad period, of a noticeable subtlety born in 640 and died in 721.

Praises

1. Avoid doing a favor to a person saturated of commanding, and overwhelmed by a political career, because he will never acknowledge any great favor you do for him. In return, he will reproach you for a small favor he did for you (Ahnaf Ibn Qaiss, 7th C.).

2. The arrogant must not claim praise, nor the one full of hatred for many friends, or the uncouth man for honor. (Alhasan Ibn Ali, 7th C.).*

3. Virtue is what the enemy recognizes. (Omar Ibn Abdal Eziz, 8-9th C.)**

4. Nothing is more meaningful to children than praises. (Omar Ibn Elkhattab).

5. Neither be carried away by praise, nor influenced by critics, because trees bloom in spring, give fruit in Summer without expecting praise, and lose their leaves in Autumn, become bare in Winter without fearing blames. (Jebran Khalil Jebran.).

➢ Differently related in English proverbs" Anger and hate hinder good counsel".

➢ Omar, the second caliph, eminent companion of the prophet Muhammad.

➢ Told otherwise in Bible proverbs: "If thine enemy be hungry, give him bread to eat; and if he be thirsty, give him water to drink".

Traditions

1. The bird gains an advantage over man because man lives in the shadows of traditions he created himself, whereas the bird lives according to the Universal law, which makes the Earth turn around the sun. (Jebran Khalil Jebran).

2. The life of a Man is a great walking procession, and from the golden dust, it raises come the languages, traditions and rituals. (Jebran Khalil Jebran).

Justice

1. In a place where a famine is ravaging, law is not respected. (Omar Ibn Al Khattab).

2. Avoid living in a country, which is not run by fair rulers. (Abdul Malik Ibn Marwan).

3. A blind law oppresses the weak when he commits a mistake, whereas it shows compassion to the strong. (Jebran Khalil Jebran.).

4. In the courts and prisons, flouted justice calls for help. (Jebran Khalil Jebran.)

5. A boss is useful as long as he is fair-minded and as long as he prevents strong people from oppressing the weaker ones. (Tales of one thousand and one nights).

Suspicion

1. Suspicion disturbs human thoughts and retards friendship. (Amru Ibn Al-Ass, 7th C)

2. Do not blame the one who suspects you if you are exposing yourself to suspicions. (Amru Ibn Al-Aass).

3. We never dissimulate something without having it appear in our speech. (Ali Ibn Abi Talib)

Caution and determination

1. If you have an opinion, try also to have a will because hesitation weakens and corrupts opinion. (Almoutanabbi, 10th century)*.

2. Show a strong personality; so that no one tries to harm you and that the weaker ones don't lose hope in your fairness. (Moauiya).

3. Like a woman, who begets a child after feeling hard pain, the soul embraces virtue only after a serious effort. (Jebran Khalib Jebran).

4. If you start a good action, don't doubt of its reward, and if you engage in a bad action, be sure that you will be reprimanded. (Ali Ibn Abi-Talib)

➢ Differently related in English proverbs "He who hesitates is lost".

---

5. He who never faces the danger shall never ride in glory, and he who is too cautious shall never achieve nobility. (Safi Alddin Alheli)*

6. Opinion comes before the bravery of the braves (Al-Moutanabi).**

7. If a wind blows, ride it. (Al Shafii)

➢ Told otherwise in English Proverbs "As you sow, so shall you reap".

➢ Al Moutanabi, one of the most famous Abaasia poet.

Knowledge

1. The one who doesn't acquire richness by knowledge at least acquires the respect of people (Alshabi 8th century).

2. Three things are lost for good: a faith without knowledge, a capacity without action, richness without generosity. (Abbasid era).*

3. The more our knowledge increases, the more our force is confirmed. (Ali Ibn Abi Talib).

4. The one who revives knowledge is not dead, and the one who possesses intelligence is not poor. (Ibn Doureid 8th century).

5. Nothing is better than living in good health and no treasure is better than knowledge. (Abbasid Era).

➢ Related otherwise in English proverbs "All things are easy that are done willingly".

---

6. A scholar who is useful to humanity is better than one thousand ascetics are. (prophet Mohammed).

7. The educator and the doctor will never be useful unless we take care of them. (Almaari).*

8. The best legacy is that of the scholar who leaves his knowledge to those who will live after him. (Abbasid Era).

9. Try hard to love science until it becomes your passion, your entertainment and your leisure. (abbasid era).

10. Try to know better and approach the scholars, be satisfied of what you have learned. Don't despise a person whose knowledge was useful to you. Everything has its significance and that of knowledge is found in the clarity of expression' Never give up knowledge because of youth or old age (Aktham Ibn Saifi, 6th century).

➤ Al'maari famous blind poet of the abbasid era of the author of the message of forgiveness "rissalatul ghoufran".

---

11. 12. know that your rank is measured according to your behavior, and that your knowledge doesn't die, and no one can steal it from you. Money disappears with time, whereas knowledge never loses its richness. (arab wisdom of Indian origin Ibn Mukaffa).

13. Try hard to learn and never ask advice to an ignorant person, even if he is sincere. (Zuheir Ibn Abi Salma 6th century).

14. The most useful thing is to consult the scholars, to acquire their experience. The most dangerous thing is laziness, an uncontrolled passion and haste. (Ali Ibn Abi Talib).*

➤ Told otherwise in American proverbs "Necessity never made a good bargain".

➤ Related by Ali Ibn Abi Talib.

Loneliness - conviviality

1. The defects of one group are better than the benefits of dispersion. (Omar bin Abdul Aziz).

2. Order close relatives to visit each other, however without living together. (Omar Ibn Al Khattab, 7th century).

3. Being distant for more than three days engenders sadness, reunion after one year renews happiness. (Yahya Ibn Khalid, 8th century).

Learning to listen

1. He who refrains from answering an ignorant person is repressing him by his silence. (Ali Ibn Abi Talib).

2. He who jokes excessively with children loses their respect. (Sanabilu al zaman, ears of time).

3. Learn to listen well as you learn to speak well: give the other the right to speak fully. Do not let him out of your eyes, and try hard to catch well what he says. (Ibn Aqil).*

4. Silence is better than debating with ignorants, break-up is better than keeping relations with nasty people. Sterility is better than having stupid children. (Ibn Abbass, 7th century).

➢ Related by Ibn Al Muqafaa.

---

5. Silence engenders dignity, whereas chattering engenders lack of respect. (Ibn Alfarid, 8th century).*

6. Silence is better than debating with ignorants, break-up is better than keeping relations with nasty people. Sterility is better than having stupid children. (Ibn Abbass, 7th century).

7. Speech is silver, but silence is gold (Al Jahez)**

➢ Told otherwise in Latin proverbs " What you want to keep secret, tell no one. If you could not control your urge to tell, how can you expect silence from".

➢ Wisdom told otherwise in English proverbs" Talk is cheap, silence is golden".

Cordiality, Friendliness

1. Earn the hearts of people and you could earn money (badaiu al zuhur, the marvels of flowers).*

2. The best of friends are those who become more interested in you when you are in difficulty. (adab al majalis, the conduct of meetings)

3. If you are a wise man, choose your house, love your wife, and embrace her, rejoice her hearts, because she is like the field, which gives flowers to those who cultivate it. (Bachar Ibn Bourd)**.

4. Happiness is like a kiss. We do not feel its softness unless we share it with others. (Adb Almajalis).

5. Satisfying all is an impossible end. (adab almajalis, the conduct of meetings)

6. Exchange gifts, and love one another. (Ali Ibn Abi Taleb).

7. He, who knows his place, will be out of danger. (Prophet Mohamed).***

➢ Differently related by Les Brown "Help others achieve their dreams and you will achieve yours".

➢ Bashar, poet of Abbasid Era, died in 784

> Told otherwise by Germaine Greer: "A successful marriage requires falling in love many times, always with the same person".

8. Maintaining good relations with relatives is a source of healthy growth of children and wealth.

9. The generous man is the one who is happy when he gives and becomes shy when he receives. Greatness is offering one's help without asking for it in return. (Abdul Malik Ibn Marwan).

10. The way of presenting an excuse reveals our greatness and dignity. (Abdul Malik Ibn Marwan).

11. Do not react to the evil someone my say about you, because the one who would hear it either supports you, or forgets it immediately for not knowing the cause. On the contrary, your reply will confirm and reveal this evil. "Soufan A".

12. Adopt new friends every day as your everlasting emblem.

13. The best quality of kings is forgiveness. (Al Muhalab Ibn Abi Jafar).

> Related by Ali Ibn Abi Talib.

Action and hope

1. Hope is a sweet companion, if it does not lead you to the goal; at least, it consoles you. (Aljahiz, 10th century)*

2. Get profits from your failures, like a ladder to climb the steps of success. (Alsibai).

3. Do not hesitate to work by fear of criticism; otherwise you won't do any thing. Do what you judge true in order to get the results that you anticipated. Hence, you shall progress in your work and your life. (Contemporary wisdom) **

4. We can bring ourselves up during our life in order not to quit it without leaving traces, which makes us eternal. (Qasim Amin, 20th century).

5. Genius is a gift that an audacious and patient man receives. (Al husein ibn Ismael)

6. Your retirement is in my heart. How would you be absent? (Jebran Khalil Jebran).

➤ told otherwise by Tom Bradley: "The only thing that will stop you from fulfilling your dreams is you".

➤ told otherwise by Thomas Edison: "our greatest weakness lies in giving up. The most certain way to succeed is always to try just one more time".

---

7. Things can be summed up this way: ordinary things which you do not have to care of, and important things which you do not have to entrust to others. If you take care of ordinary things, they won't leave you enough time for important things. If you entrust important things to others, you will lose more than you achieve. (Ali Ibn Abi Talib)

8. God wants you to perfect what you do. (Prophet Mohamed)*

9. Seek your livelihood in the bottom of the Earth. (Prophet Mohamed).

10. Do not give way to sadness, it shrinks the heart and chases away hope. Sadness does not bring any advantage and know that if you accomplish a serious work of which you are not certain, it will surely make a sensation among others.

11. Be a force in your work or in your knowledge. This is the real pleasure. (Ahmed Showki)**

➤ Related in another way in German proverbs "The action has a mightier impact than the word".

➤ Ahmed Showki one of the most famous Egyptian poet (20th century).

---

12. Take the opportunity and try to acquire different experiences. You don't know which experience will be useful to you one day.

13. Don't fear mistakes, the fear of committing a mistake gives more occasions to its occurrence.

14. Don't try to take any decision when you are tired or when you are under pressure.

15. Fear of failure is the lack of attempting. (Mohamed Abdu)

16. Great hopes generate great deeds. (Marazem Bin Haqim).

17. If you don't have hopes, create them for yourself.

18. Don't let praise or criticism changes your will.

19. Sadness is not the fact of not achieving your hopes, but is the fact of not having any hope at all.

Moderation

1. If you love do not go beyond the limits, and if you hate do not do it excessively. (Hisham Ibn Abdul Malek).*

2. The one who asks more than what he deserves will know deprivation. (Ibin Shaddad 7th century).

3. The vice engendered by destitution is more bearable than the vice engendered by richness. (Abu Zar Al gefari)**

4. The one who exaggerates in polemics and the one who gives up are wrong. (Ali Ibn Abi Talib). ***

5. If you want to get what you wish, try to wish for only what you can get. (Ali Ibn Abi Talib)

6. Know that each person possesses some vices and virtues and that the vices of a man must not prevent you to profit from his virtues. (Abu Hureira.7th century).

➢ told otherwise in French proverbs : " When we cannot get what we love, we must love what is within our reach".

➢ Differently related in American proverbs" It is less of a problem to be poor, than to be dishonest".

> ➤ Told in another way in Latin Proverbs: "Anger is the one thing made better by delay".

---

7. If we ask those who rest in their tombs what was the cause of their death, they would reply: "We had eaten greedily. (Talha ibn Obeid Allah).

8. Eating to repletion causes headache, sight troubles and indigestion. So eat moderately and beware of eating food at night. (All Shafie).

9. The one who seeks fast tranquility will never get it, the one who submits to his passion will stay deprived of his force. (prophet Mohamed)*.

10. If you are quarrelling, keep to equity, and be moderate when you lose your temper. (Alhassan Bin Ali).

11. If you know how to swim well, do not rush to the bottom of the valley. **

> ➤ Told in another way in Kalila and Dimna

> ➤ Contemporary wisdom, of which the origin can be traced back to Persian wisdom (Abbasid Era)

Destitution and richness

1. The only difference between the poor and the rich is that the first is anxious of his next meal, whereas the latter has not yet got over his last meal. (Alhassan Albasri, 10th century).

2. Money conceals the vices of rich people, whereas destitution covers the virtues of poor people. (Ali Ibn Abi Talib)*

3. You cannot help all people with your possessions, but you may serve them through your joy and high morality. (Prophet Mohamed).

4. The destitution of a generous man is better than the richness of a stingy man, and an unlucky wise man is better than a lucky stupid one. (Abbassid Era)

5. Do not consult a poor man even if you are confident in his friendship.

➢ Told in another way in African proverb: "The poor man and the rich man do not play together." by Buzzie Bavasi. "Those who have the gold make the rules".

---

6. The one who loses his possessions shall lose gradually the respect of his family. (Netajul Fitna, the consequences of sagacity).

7. Four things kill a man before his time: destitution, corruption of children, bad morals and the loss of friends. (Ali Ibn Abi Talib)*.

8. A person shall never be poor as long as he is not suffering from three things: lack of faith, reason and morality. (Ali Ibn Abi Talib).**

9. The best man is the one who behaves modestly despite his greatness, with sobriety despite his richness, and with equity despite his strength. (Ali Ibn Abi Talib).

10. Do not underestimate money and its investment, because money is a means in itself to accomplish noble actions and constitutes a support in life, a force to pay off debts and a means to make friends.

➢ Told in another way in Spanish proverbs: "A wise son makes his father glad, but a foolish son is a grief to his mother".

➢ Was pronounced in another way by: Joseph Addison "The greatest sweetener of human life is Friendship,To raise this to the highest pitch of enjoyment, is a secret which but few discover"

---

11. poverty causes disdain, lack of respect and consideration. Each person that people neither

fear nor envy will find himself despised by others. (Arab wisdom of Indian origin Kalila and Dimna).

12. A hard life of a dignified person is better than an easy life of a corrupt one. (Al-Maamoun).

13. He who expects death will be fully committed to accomplish good deeds. (Ibnu Arabi, 8th century).

14. The ways of salvations are three: honesty, piety and a healthy diet. (Abdul Malik Ibn Marwan).

15. We asked a wise man: "what is the most pleasant life"? he replied: "a comfortable life with neither poverty nor richness." (Ibn Salam, 8th Century).

16. People will stay faithful to you as long as you do not become poor. (Amoukhtar – the elected).

17. The more we get rich, the more we become anxious.

18. If you want to blame your friend, act by doing him good, and react to his wrongdoing with beneficence. (Ali Ibn Abi Taleb).

19. If your friend commits a mistake, try to find an excuse for him. (Alahnaf Ibn Qais)

20. It is not of the habit of nobles to take their revenge on the spot. (Alhassen Ibn Ali).

21. The most rational of men is the one who tries to justify the actions of others. (Ali Ibn Abi Talib).

22. When you are angry lie down on your back, and when you are tired raise up you legs. (Ibn Habaryia, 11th Century).

23. try to ransom your enemy and get a little closer to him, so not to give him the occasion to harm you. But do not approach him too much for the fear that he offends you. (Omar Ibn Abdelaziz, 7-8th Cent.)*

24. The most courageous man is the one who learns how to control him self. (prophet Mohamed).

➢ Told in another way in Bible proverbs: "If thine enemy be hungry, give him bread to eat; and if he be thirsty, give him water to drink".

Satisfaction

1. The one who is pleased with what he has leads a happy life. (Alhassen Ibn Abi Talib)

2. If a man owns two valleys full of wealth, he wishes a third one. (prophet Mohamed).

3. How many people on this Earth have left us suddenly, without taking anything with them? (Abu Alatalyia, 10th Cent.)*

4. Behind pleasures, troubles are hidden, and the best pleasure is the tranquility of the soul. (Abu Alaswad Eddwali 7th Cent)*

5. A free man becomes a slave if he is stingy, and the slave becomes free if he is satisfied with the little he possesses (Alhassen Ibn Ali).

6. If you want to be rich try to satisfy yourself reasonably with what you own because an unsatisfied man will never be rich, whatever his fortune. (Alhassen Ibn Ali).

➢ Told in another way in Kalila and Dimna

---

7. A man can see a woman at a distance and thinks she is most attractive, but it happens that he is

disappointed when he comes close to her. (Speech related to love and women).

8. Do not feel like all what you hear about. (Ali Ibn Abi Taleb)

9. A wise man must never be sad about things he lacks in this life. He must consider things acquired and lost thereafter as never having been obtained. (Ibn Ghourra, 8th, Century).

10. People's affairs can be summarized into three categories: knowledge, sobriety, and justice. (Ibn Abass)

11. The one who gets satisfied is rich even if he is hungry and undressed, the stingy remains poor even while possessing all wealth on earth. (Alhassen Ibn Ali).

12. Three things maintain pain: excessive miserliness, insistent begging, and envious wishes. (Abdellah Ibn Masoud).

Frankness - lying

1. The man who lies loses self-respect. (Ali Ibn Abi Taleb).

2. He who confesses you frankly his enmity reveals his noble traits. (Omar Ibn Abdelaziz).

3. He who denounces his vices, succeeds in correcting them. (Ali Essalami, 12th Cent).

4. Four are ashamed: The liar, the newsmonger, the one in debt, and the poor. (Ali Ibn Abi Talib)

5. You may lose your friend, if you frankly tell what you think of him. (Ibn Arabi).

6. The one, who tells you what people say about you, will tell people what you say about them. (Outhman Ibn Affane)*

7. A compatriot praising himself, was asked; Why? He replied, "Would I leave it to an enemy who would blame me?"

8. A man criticizing himself openly is praising himself secretly.

➢ Third caliph, companion of the prophet

Husbands

1. If you see a man opening the car's door for his wife, be sure that one of the two is new. (Hakki)

2. Man is the chandelier who lights the house. If he dies, the tears light it. (Almoutewakill)

3. A man must not have conjugal relations with his wife when he is sad, anxious, worried, busy, angry, or drunk. (Alshaabi, 8th Cent.)*.

> ➤ Ashaabi Ibn Humaid (630-771), very ugly comedian of the Umayyad era.

Education

1. Do not compel your children to copy your conduct because they are born to live in an era different from yours. (Ali Ibn Abi Talib - born in Mecca died in 661AD).

2. Be to your students as an immaculate mirror. Avoid some habits, which encourage them not to respect you. Never share secrets with them and show rightness. Teach them to despise miserliness and excess. (Arab wisdom of Persian origin).

3. Do not look at the beauty of the face, but rather the dignity of actions. (Arab wisdom of Persian origin).

4. The child who draws sad forms expresses with his pen what cannot be said orally. (Soufan. A).

5. Relax so that there will be no roughness in your religion. (prophet Mohamed)*

6. The best place in the world is on the back of a horse, and the best friend in all time is a book. (Almoutanabbi, 10th century)

➢ Pronounced by Ali Ibn Abi Taleb.

Morality

1. Nations are worth by their morality. If morality goes away, nations follow. (Ahmed Chawki 19-20).

2. Martyrs are those who died for their country, their principles or their fellows, and the best among them are those who generated great ideas, anticipating over their time, thus working for the good of humanity.

3. The least intelligent man is the one who harms his neighbor. (Almamoun)*

4. Politeness embellishes fortune for richer men, and hides the destitution of the poorer ones.

5. Do not intervene when a man speaks about something you already know, in order not to hurt him, because that belongs to impoliteness and weak-mindedness. (Al Hussein Ibn Ali).

6. Do not argue with your family members even if you feel eloquent. (Ibn Abbass).

➢ Told in another way in American proverbs" Do not wrong or hate your neighbor for it is not he that you wrong but yourself ".

---

7. Avoid cheating in business; avoid arrogance and submission, because the scholar does not let himself be influenced by windfalls nor by difficulties and dangers. (Ibn Haroun)*

8. I would rather die of thirst than to miss an appointment. (Almouthana Ibn Khaja).

9. He who needs me has to write it down, so that he avoids coming and asking it to me with humiliation. (Ali Ibn Abi Talib).

10. Respect yourself first. It is the easiest way to be respected by others, and respect the seniors in the service with kindness.

11. Be polite if you are a King, you will be safe! If you are in the middle, you will get higher; if you are poor you will become richer. (Ibn Akariya).

➢ Ibn Haron, Souhail, the master of the wisdom treasure in the time of caliph Almamoun, Abbasid Era -10thcentury.

Courage

1. The most beautiful thing is that man never fears death, as he must not fear life. (Ibnul Amid, 11th century)*.

2. Do not fear death because pain lies in the fear of facing it. (Al-Ahnaf Ibn Qais)**

3. The wise man must not sow disagreement by a well educated scholar, does not let himself be excited by benefits nor influenced by difficulties. (Ali Ibn Abi Talib).

➢ Ibn Alamid was nicknamed Ajakhiz for knowledge. Man of letter in the Abbasid era.

➢ Was pronounced by Ibn Alarabi

Friendship

1. If you want to be a friend with someone, manage to irritate him first, if he reacts with equity towards you, adopt him, if not, keep away from him. (Ali Ibn Abi Talib).

2. How many brothers do you have to whom your mother did not beget? (Prophet Mohammed).

3. The best thing a man can acquire is a faithful friend and a compassionate wife. (Arab wisdom-Kalila and Dimna).*

4. The good actions and the qualities of a person exist and develop only owing to real friends. (Abu Darda).

5. A friendship with a silly one raised among wise men is better than a friendship with an intelligent one raised among ignorant. (Arab wisdom from Persian origin)

6. You must give love and obedience to the one who pays you a sincere friendship and good advice. (Bashar Ibn Burd, 8th century)*

➢ Related in another way By Baltasar Gracian "Friendship multiplies the good of life and divides the evil".

---

7. Know that too much of criticism leads to the break-up, and absence of reproach is a sign of lack of interest done to a friend. So, be moderate: focus your blames on the things which you share advantages and drawbacks, and give no importance to details in order to save your friendship. (Aljahiz).

8. All familiarity is not necessarily a friendship, all retire within oneself is not necessarily a refusal of friendship. (Arab wisdom of Persian origin).

9. The best thing a man can do for his friends is to enquire about their problems and in case of need, help them as far as he can without pushing them to begging. And if they trespass, he continues visiting their children. If it happens that he makes himself known, everyone will like to have him as a friend; and thus he shall have satisfied his conscience. (Beshar Ibn Bourd).

10. Some qualities, which allow knowing serene friends: hide their defects, speak to them about what they like, and avoid evoking what they hate. (Arab wisdom of Persian origin).

➢ Related in another way in Danish proverbs "The road to a friend's house is never too long"

---

11. The heart of a friend is a fragile thing of which you have to be careful, because like glass once broken cannot be put back together again. (Tales of one thousand and one nights).*

12. Do not be afraid of a person you distrust, but beware from a person in whom you put your trust. (Arab wisdom of Persian origin).

13. Among the things, which ease worries and keep the mind serene: the meeting between two brothers when each one of them reveals his concerns to the other?

14. Do not be afraid of a person you distrust, but beware from a person in whom you put your trust. (Arab wisdom of Persian origin).

15. Among the things, which ease worries and keep the mind serene: the meeting between two brothers when each one of them reveals his concerns to the other?

➢ This part is found in Kelila and Dimna as speech of animals

---

Obstinacy

1. You can crush a flower, but how can you tear out its perfume? (Jebran Khalil Jebran)*

2. How numerous are those who are used to the specters of their ancestors, like caverns in the deserted valleys, which send echoes without understanding their meaning. (Jebran Khalil Jebran).

3. Why do two brothers fight over the breast of their own mother? Why does the cross move away from the crescent under the eye of one God? (Jebran Khalil Jebran).

4. If man thinks for one moment that he was with all men on the same vessel and that religions constitute the same family since Moses, Jesus, and Mohamed; people will like each others more, and be unified in front of their unique Creator. (Jebran Khalil Jebran).

5. Avoid foolish anger, because it will oblige you afterward to ask for an apology.

6. You are hammering on cold iron (Abu Al shamqiq 730- 815)**

➤ contemporary wisdom, of which the origin can be traced back to Persian wisdom (Abbasid Era)

> ➤ Was pronounced in another way in German proverbs "Strike while the iron is hot".

Pride and modesty

1. Do not bear pride's burden and know what you do without going beyond the limits. Fear your fathers, take care of your mothers, and do not answer a question, which is not addressed to you. Do not speak up to persons elder than you; and avoid quarreling with them. (from the Abbasid Era)*.

2. do not be concerned with others' vices; do not consider yourself a wise man. It is for the others to acknowledge your wisdom. Do not be proud; do not brag of your properties, your supremacy or of your victories over your rivals. (Alhassan Ibn Ali)**

3. If a person honors you, be modest. If you are entrusted with doing a job, do it well. Control your anger remains dignified. Do not claim having what you cannot reach. (Abdullah Ibn Massoud, 7th Cent.).

4. Try your best to be modest among the people, this does not demean you, on the contrary, it will raise you in their eyes and it will avoid you to speak first. (Abbasid Era).

➤ Taken from a hadith (prophet's tradition) and a part from Kelila and Dimna.

➤ The first part in Kelila and Dimna as animal speech.

Honor

1. Man must try hard to be always dignified when he finds himself in front of two situations, one which brings many materialistic benefits and another which brings much dignity. He must seize the occasion to promote his social rank, because the importance of the place he is occupying will necessarily allow him to earn some money, whereas money does not necessarily allow him to occupy a social position. It is very useful to man to satisfy his needs by his rank and not by his money. (Ibn Safwan, 8th century, Nuzhtul Hukama).

2. The one who intercedes for someone and accepts his present is committing a sin (prophet Mohamed).

Beneficence and charity

1. The one who accomplishes a good deed to someone must not remind him of it, and never forget the one who does you a good deed. (Almaari)*

2. Three things are necessary for doing the good: to do it without hesitation, to consider it modest be it great, and avoid to boasting of it in front of the beneficiary. (Arab wisdom of Parisian origin).

3. A benefactor does not do the good in favor of the good ones and leaves the bad ones, but he is the one who does it for all. (Ghaiss Ibn Assim 8th century) **

➢ Related in Romanien proverbs.

➢ Arab wisdom of Indian origin from Kelila and Dimna.

Greatness of the soul

1. the perfect man is the one who has nothing to hide and does not fear of divulging anything. (Ali Ibn Abi Talib).

2. Do not backbite the absents, do not swear in order to convince people, do not laugh constantly, know how to control yourself, avoid magic, and do not speak of others' vices. (Arab wisdom from Parisian origin).*

➢   Related in another way By Yazid bin Moawia.

Perfection

1. Place fear and hope where they must be. Drive out immediate passions and bear the imminent boredom so that you can avoid the one, which stands at the horizon. (Akthem Ibn Saifi).

2. With wisdom we discover knowledge, with satisfaction life becomes happy, with reason we reach the summits, with misfortune appear the virtues of humankind.

3. After a long absence, we discover the welcome of friends, and at the moment of anger we discover the integrity of men. (Arab wisdom from Parisian origin).

4. The one who behaves humbly covers his vices. (Arab wisdom from Parisian origin)

5. A wise man gave advice to his son: "try to be abstentious in order to reach satisfaction and the tranquility of the soul, be a hard-worker and you will get what you aspire for, and you will get security (Arab wisdom from Parisian origin).

6. 7. Your opinion must be based on true knowledge, and your knowledge on strong arguments, embellish your speech by truth. Let your gifts be lavished with generosity. (From Abbasid era).

8. the real joy : "A reason which highlights you, a knowledge serving you as adornment, a child who pleases you, a security which gives you tranquility, a health which gathers all the sources of joy (Al Hussein Bin Ali).

9. Men are of the same nature, and can be differentiated from one another only by their external appearance. (Jebran Khalil Jebran)*

> ➢ Related in another way in American proverbs "
> With all things and in all things, we are relatives".
> (Sioux)

---

10. "If you advise someone against a thing, advise yourself first against it, if you quarrel with someone be fair with him, if you speak moderate your speech, (Ibn Said Hassan, 7th century).

11. Bloodshed is forbidden, who has allowed it to the judges? (Jebran Khalil Jebran).*

12. If you have no shame then do whatever you want (Prophet Mohamed 7th century).

13. The purest people are the ones with good manners (Prophet Mohamed 7th century).

> ➢ Told otherwise in Latin proverbs "Who will watch the watchmen"?

Behavior

1. We asked a wise man: "How must we behave towards ourselves, our Sultan, our parents and friends?", he replied: toward yourself, deploy a sustainable effort, towards the Sultan, provide him good advice, towards parents love them and never neglect them, towards friends beneficence and bring them consolation at the appropriate time. (Ajahiz).

2. The one, who wants to enjoy a good reputation, must try his best to have good morals and put himself in the service of others by good actions. (Partially told in Kalila and Dimna).*

3. Accept from others only what you accept for yourself, and do not make promises that you cannot keep (Partially told in Kalila and Dimna).

4. Avoid quarrels and enmities because they often come from a simple joke or a lack of reservation (From the Abbasid era).

5. The problems of sons is what they inherit from their fathers and the one who relies on his ancestors' heritage remains a slave to the dead until he himself dies (Speech Related to women and love).

➢ Told otherwise in Bible proverbs: "Hatred stirs up disputes, but love covers all offenses".

Various

1. In schools and offices, hopeless youth is calling upon you, in the houses of cult you will be attracted by neglected books. (Jebran Khalil Jebran).

2. Do not insult others and do not drive away a beggar. If he is good, you should have helped him, if he is a poor devil, you would have not given him the occasion to say evil things about you. (Hatim Ataai 6th century)

3. Habits are alienating. The one who is used to a thing in secret, that thing will deceive him in public. (Sanabel Al zaman)

4. One reaches his goal by the quality of his speech and the worry of not offending. (Ahmed Chawki).

5. Four things are destructive for man: the immoderate love of women, gambling, hunting and alcohol.

6. Do not regret the fact of not being rich because money comes as quick as it goes. (Ibn Safwan, 8th century, Nuzhatul Hukama).

7. Six things are worth the whole life: a healthy food, a clement master, an obedient son, a compassionate wife, good sense and sound reasoning. (Ibn Safwan).

8. Know that eating a lot, sleeping a lot and having bad habits are considered like drunkenness, whereas happiness is linked to reason and moderation (From Abbasid Era).

9. Be discrete in your business in order to avoid problems. Man must necessarily consult the noble, the ambitious, and the wise because these people do not divulge secrets. (Ibn Salam, 8th century).

10. The best of speech is that of the truth and the best deed is that of generosity.

11. The worst speech is lying; and the worst deed is miserliness" (Arab Wisdom Abbasid Era).

12. Kinship requires friendliness whilst friendliness doesn't require kinship. (Aktham Ibn Saifi, 6th Cent)

13. Every thing has its reason .The reason of a happy life is to know how to treat people and this requires a particular insight. The reason of fraternity is a smiling face. The reason of ruin is anger. The reason of break-up is the multiplication of reproaches. (Abbasid era)

14. I have tasted every kind of good things and I haven't found anything better than good health. (Ali Ibn Abi Talib).

15. Happiness never happens before experiencing an adventure or certain courage, and spontaneous words push our potential and noble forces to discover a radiant sun.

16. Between the kings and me there is one day: they have not found the taste of yesterday. (Abbu Hazem).

17. They and I, we feared that next day. We have the day of today, but what will happen tomorrow? (Abu Hazem).

18. You who complain without suffering of illness, what will be of you tomorrow when you become sick? (Ilia Abu-Madhi).

19. Carelessness is the Cemetry of the vice. (Abu Hazem).

20. The fruit of insistence is the torment, the one of hastiness is the regret, and the one of vanity is hatred. (Aktham Bin Saifi, 6th Cent).

21. Keeping secrets is the sign of worthy men. (Al Muhallab)

22. The sea has no neighborhood, the king has no friends, and peace has no price. (Abdul Malik Ibn Marwan).*

23. 24. Whoever advises his friend secretly pleases and embellishes him and whoever advises his

friend openly displeases and dishonors him. (Ummu Darda, 7th century).

25. The anger of the ignorant lies in his speech, of the wise in his deed. (Nahj Al Balagha, Rhetoric method).

➤ Wisdom told other wise in English & Spanish proverbs "Worse things happened at sea."

Proverbs

Introduction to Arab proverbs

The Arab proverbs were subject to modifications after which several of them have known different readings, in view that they constituted the kind of speech the most widespread among people and the most commonly used in the language.

If the wisdoms have thrived in the caliphs and sultans cabinet following the example of poetry, and was linked to power and the regime, the Arab proverbs had for origin the Arabs who lived in the countryside and are in close contact with all sorts of animals.

If the change has ruined some ancient Arab books, the biggest part was that of proverbs and wisdom (*). Each proverb has a story. But who is the one that knows the story of each proverb, a mainly ancient proverbs coming from remote eras.

> ➢ Ahmed Amin (Fajru Il-Islam, the Dawn of Islam).

It is known that a proverb may come from an incident, from a metaphor, from a story or an extract of poetry. We have chosen a bouquet of ancient proverbs of pure Arabic language, which recalls briefly an incident or a story. We made sure to present to the reader an example of a story already mentioned at the end of each proverb.

1. 2. Give the bow to his sharpener.*

3. Oil in the paste is never lost. **

4. Nothing is closer to a man than his shadow.

5. Beauty lies in the speech

6. Criticism precedes punishment.

7. It is better to rebuke ones' brothers than lose them. ***

8. It is a good shooting that of a bad shooter. (Abu Darda) ****

9. A problem is solved when it gets tougher. (Abu Al Fadl Al Nuzari-12th century).

10. He behaves as lion towards me and is an ostrich in war. (Omran Al Ṣadoussi 7th century).

➢ Proverbs from Jahilya era before Islam (100-600 AD).

➢ Reported in African proverbs.

➢ Differently related by Samuel Butler: "Friendship is like money, easier made than kept".

➢ Wisdom told other wise in English proverb "Things are not always what they seem".

---

11. News come from where you least expect it. (Turfa Ibn Al Abd).*

12. A farmer for himself, his harvest for the others. (Ali Ibn Abi Talib)

13. A slaughtered animal suffers no more.

14. A satiated person cooks slowly for a hungry one.

15. To throw one's buckets among the buckets is to make one's voice heard in the concert.

16. The one who fears the duel will never succeed**.

17. More numerous than ants,

18. Tighter than a needle's eye.

19. Softer than dawn sleeping.

> ➤ Wisdom told other wise in Bible proverbs " As cold waters to a thirsty soul, so is good news from a far country ".

> ➤ Proverbs from Jahilya era before Islam (100-600 AD) – Differently related in Japonaise proverbs.

20. More cautious than the chameleon.

21. More stupid than an Ostrich.

22. More dangerous than a scorpion.

23. Make your visit short and you will be appreciated.*

24. Need engenders the means.**

25. I hear a crackle, but I do not see a flour .

26. A needle in a haystack.

27. A husband of wood, and not a dromedary. (Al Isba Al Idwani girl).

28. Each girl admires her father. (Almoustakssi).

> ➤ Related in another way in Enlish proverbs " A constant guest is never welcome".

> ➤ Related in another way in Spanish proverbs" Necessity is the mother of invention".

Middle East Common proverbs

1. Who trust men are like water in the riddle.

2. Close your door and secure your neighbor.

3. The mind is a decoration.

4. A good name is better than riches

5. A bird in the hand is better than a pigeon on the three.*

6. Cat your coat according to your cloth.

7. Every decayed grain of wheat has a one eyed corn measurer.

8. Smoke of the neighbours renders you blind

➤ Related in another way in German proverbs" "A sparrow in the hand is better than a pigeon on the roof".

---

9. If you are a prince and so am I, Who will lead the donkeys?

10. Among the blind, the one-eyed man is king.*

11. Do well and throw it in the sea.

12. Save your white penny for your black day

13. Like father, like son. **

14. People are enemies of that which they don't know.

15. Too much coquetry makes the lover escape.

16. Beat the iron while it is hot ***

17. Easy come easy go.

18. Don't sleep in the cemetery, and complain from nightmares.

➢ related in in another way in German proverbs " The blind man explains the colors to the one-eyed man".

➢ related in German & Enlish proverbs " Like father, like son".

➢ Wisdom told in Spanish & Enlish proverbs" You have to strike while the iron is hot".

---

19. Nothing is better to scrub your skin than your own nail.

20. When we traded with coffins, people ceased to die.

21. From outside a marble, and inside mud.

22. Visit people in the morning and not in the evening.

23. When poverty comes in at the door , love flies out of the window.

24. Birds of a feather flock together.

25. A man is known by the company he keeps.

26. Too many hands spoil the sauce.*

27. Silence gives consent

28. He wanted to make-up the eye, and he blinded it

➢ Related in English proverbs

---

29. The vinegar worms are not alike.

30. A borrowed thing does not keep warm.

31. More vulnerable than a spider's web.

32. A cat has seven lives.*

33. A mountain does not go to meet a mountain; a man goes to meet a man.

34. When the cat is away, mice play.

35. I taught him archery everyday, and when he got good at it he throw an arrow at me. (Imru' al-Qais) **

36. People follow the winner.

37. A hungry stomach has no ears.

38. The last straw that broke the camels back.

❯ Related in English Proverbs

❯ Imru' al-Qais - Amr Ibn Muawya- Pre-Islamic Period –Aljahiliya.

---

39. If your friend is of honey, don't snap up it all.

40. The monkey in his mother's eye is a gazelle*

41. Whoever envies the monkey for his possession, soon the properties will vanish, and the monkey remains the same..

42. Single for an era and not a widow for one month

43. Those who are far from the eye are far from the heart **

44. If you are associated with someone, associate only with princes, and if you steal, don't steal but silk.

45. Take the genuine even if it is on the mat.

46. The door of the carpenter is taken out. ***

47. A rolling stone gathers no moss.

❯ Related in another way in Japanese proverbs."

❯ Reported other wise in Spanish proverbs "If you leave your place, you lose it".

➢ Wisdom told other wise in English proverbs "The shoemaker's son always goes barefoot".

---

48. Tougher than a stone.

49. Where the wind comes, bulge it and rest.

50. If you are taken away by the wind, you will meet a cyclone.

51. People, who live in glass houses, shouldn't throw stones.*

52. To make mountains out of molehills

53. No one will confess that his oil is turbid.

54. The people's lord is their servant.

55. Whoever eats the Sultan's bread must defend him with his sword.

56. When the cow falls down, there will be a lot of knives.

57. Luck in the sky and brains in the ground.

➢ Related in Spanish proverbs

---

58. The village's piper does not exhilarate.

59. Each cock crows on his own dunghill.*

60. The property which is not in your homeland is neither for you, nor for your son.

61. The idea came after the drunkness passed away.

62. He beated me and cried, and run before me to complain.

63. Your close neighbor and not your far brother.

64. Feed the mouth, the eye becomes shy.

65. My husband wants me strong, my family wants me rich and my neighbors want me generous.

66. Water belies the diver.

67. You left them lost and bewildered (Abu Ja'far El Mansour 8th).

➢ Related in English Proverbs.

---

68. The rope of lying is short.

69. The bird flees and the hunter complains.

70. Don't put your head in the lions mouth. (Abu Habbat Al Numeiri).

71. When your son grows up, become his brother.

72. He is no mans enemy but his owm. (Omar Al Ansei 1821-1876).

73. He is not a wise man, who plays the fool on occasion. (Abu Tamam – 803-845).

74. A drowing man will catch at a straw.*

75. Give the bread dough to the baker even if he eats half of it.**

76. I'm already drowning so why should I fear getting wet? (Almoutanabi).***

77. Continue to do good deeds, even if you are leaving your neighborhood

---

➢ Related in English Proverbs

➢ Reported other wise in Japonaise proverbs.

➢ Almoutanabi, one of the most famous Abdasia poet

Anecdotes

1. While I was walking in a valley, I passed by a rock on which was in scripted: Oh, lovers, in the name of God, tell me if a young person falls in love what does he do? Alasmaii wrote under it: "He conceals his love, keeps his secret and behaves with reverence and submission". Alasmaii came back the day after and found written under his own inscription: "Can he conceal his love while it is killing him, and every day cuts his heart into pieces?" he wrote under it "If he cannot afford to keep his secrets, he has nothing better than death." He came back the day after and found written under it: "We heard and complied with, and then we died, please transmit our sincere greetings to those who prevented our meetings".
   (T. Alasmaii's anecdote)

2. An amusing anecdote from the Abbasid era:* "A man married a woman after divorcing another, the divorced one passed by the house of the new one and said: 'The two clothes are not the same, a shabby cloth and a new cloth between the seller's hands; then the new spouse passed by the door of the older one and said 'Displace your heart whenever you want love, because love is only for the first lover.'**

➢ Was pronounced in another way in German proverbs: "Old love does not rust".

➢ Sample of a tale in Jahilya era before Islam, Al Maydani.

3. I am addressing you, listen to me, Oh the most beautiful among the beautiful! A man was on a trip, went through an oasis inhabited by peasants and he asked to meet their chief. They showed him where he usually lived but he was not there. The chief's sister offered him hospitality; she was hidden behind her veil. She welcomed him very warmly and spoke in a soft voice words he never heard before. He discovered her beauty, and failed deeply in love with her. He asked her to marry him: "Oh, the most beautiful of the countries and cities, look at me" he said. The young woman heard what he said and understood that he was addressing her and told him: "stay as long as you like and go whenever you like, I will never reproach you". (Alghazari Souhail, 5th century).

- 5 -

Excerpts from Jewish, Kurdish, And Far East Wisdom

5 - 1
Jewish Wisdom

1. Whoever gets married in the darkness, divorces in the daylight?

2. The house of someone is his wife.*

3. The father is domination, the uncle is a distress, the brother is a trap, the child is a pain and the relatives are scorpions.

4. If poor men get married, beggars increase. **

5. If a rich man steals, we say that he is mistaking, when a poor man is mistaking, we say that he steals.

6. A disturbing truth is better than a suitable lie.

7. When reporting the speech of some one, imagine him standing in front of you.

➤ Differently related by Bashar Ibn Burd, poet of Abbasid Era, died in 784

➤ Wife is like the field, which gives flowers to those who cultivate it.

➤ Wisdom told other wise in Arabic & Indian wisdoms "poverty causes disdain, lack of respect and consideration. Each person that people neither fear nor envy will find himself despised by others".

---

8. Two things cannot stay long hidden: richness and poverty.

9. If the poor is courageous, we say that he is a reckless; if he is eloquent, we say that he is talkative.

10. Exile in richness is a homeland; the homeland in poverty is an exile.

11. Richness and knowledge are like roses and narcissus, which never bloom together.

12. Words coming from the heart enter the heart.

13. He who saves the life of a man saves the life of humanity.

14. The strong man is the one who knows how to control his desires.*

➤ Differently relatedin   in   Arabic proverbs"
The weakness of man appears when a woman
starts wooing him". (Speech related to love and
women).

---

5 - 2
Excerpts from of the
Kurdish Wisdom

The wisdom and the proverbs constitute a component of the common man, folk, and so, the intellectual and social patrimony of the Kurdish and French speaking people were able to discover this patrimony through a book written by a Kurdish writer Emir Karman Badr and the French writer Paul Margret in a book entitled Proverbs and Wisdom of Eastern people published by "the Printing" *

The book contains more than 350 proverbs and Kurdish wisdom. The Kurdish wisdom is spread in many Arab and foreign books.

Samir Khane Abdoulah Alsindi, the Kurdish wisdom, Ministry of Information and Culture, Baghdad, 1979. P 23- 33

Experiences

1. Do not judge watermelon by its color.

2. One question leads to another.

3. Lean your head against old walls.

4. Ask advice to the whole world then do what you think is best.

5. Be the owner and never the partner.

6. If you catch him do not leave him and if you leave him, try not to catch him.

7. If someone tells you that your head is uncovered, put your hands on your head (The respect from the point of view of the community.)*

8. A boy can become a prince, but a girl can became a mother.

➢ Dr. Mahmoude Ghoura, Ears of Time, Nawval Institution,Beirut, Lebanon, 1993.

---

9. 10. The lion dies, but its skin remains (the good deeds of a person last after his death.).

11. An old man is not observed by his advanced age, but rather by his way of living, (the effect of the way

of living is despair or optimism on people despite the passage of time).

12. The enemy of the father never becomes a friend of the son.

13. Life is like a rose, which changes its color perpetually. (Samir Khan Abdulla Alsindi-Global wisdom).

Action

1. The place where we find the means of living is the place we should live in.

2. A common pot will never give a good meal.

3. The longest finger tastes the honey.

4. We hear the roar of a mill but there is no flour."

5. Perseverance is source of richness, whereas idleness is source of bankruptcy.

➢ Related in Arabic wisdoms * I hear a crackle, but I do not see a flour.

---

5 - 3
Chinese Wisdom

1. The eyes of others are what our eyes see, and the ears of others are the windows of our sins.

2. The happy man is the one who knows that he is happy.

3. The house where the hen plays the role of the cock is doomed to failure.

4. Beautiful girls are not always happy and clever boys are not always handsome.

5. Lapidate woman with precious stones.

6. If you pronounce a word it becomes your master and

7. If you ride on the back of the leopard, you will not easily know how to come down.

8. Whoever goes to court earns a cat and loses a cow.

9. Lying does not have a foot, whereas scandals have wings.

10. An intelligent man loves a naïve woman.

5 - 4
Far East Wisdom

1. Make a drawing of a tree's branch and you will hear the noise of the wind (Japanese wisdom).

2. Only one nice word might have wonderful consequences (Japanese Wisdom).

3. Cowards die many times before their death (Japanese Wisdom).

4. A woman is like a raindrop, no one knows whether it will fall in a palace or in the mud of rich fields (Vietnamese wisdom).

5. It is easier to live with an intelligent man than to live with an intelligent woman. (Russian wisdom)

6. When money speaks, truth remains silent.

7. We test gold with fire and we test men with money. (Russian wisdom)*

8. The guest becomes gold, then silver, then iron. (Russian wisdom)

> ➤ Rrelated in Chinese poverbs.

Bibliography of the Main Authors

1. Kalila and Dimna wrote Indian fables, which dramatize animals. These were translated in 13th century into ancient Spanish, then to Hebrew by Goel, a religious Jew, then were translated into Latin and after to Europeans language. They were translated into Arabic by Ibnul Moqaffa' a in the 8th century.

2. La Penjatentra – A series of Indian tales dramatizing animals (fables) concerning the art of governing, These are different in Kalila and Dimna by the fact that freedom of speech when speaking about kings was more obvious in La Penjatentra, and it was limited in Kalila and Dimna.

3. Ibnul Mouquaffa'a (159-724) was born in Fayrouzabad in Persia. He lived during the period of Omeyyades and Abbasids. We owe to him the translation into Arabic of fables Bidpai Kalila & Dimna that have fed Arabic literature many tales, proverbs and sayings. He has also translated a treatise on the art of governing and gathered authentic wisdom and proverbs, taken from ancient Indian wisdom.

4. Taghour (1861-1941) was au Indian poet who received The Noble Prize in 1913 Ronal Roman, after having met him in Paris said: You feel when approaching him as if you were in a church speaking in a low voice of an attractive personality who has an appearance of pride. Tranquility threads its way through the features of his face, which hides a sad look of frustrated feelings and springs out the intelligence of man, which gives him the force to face life with stoicism.

5. AL Chirazi Saadi. Was born in Chiraz in 1120. He lived 90 years, and was one of the most famous Persian poets. His poetry was distinguished by its deep meaning and its beautiful style. We owe to him many sayings and wisdom.

6. Alzamakhchari, born in Khawarizm (between Turkmenistan and Uzbekistan) in 1074 died in

1173. He was a philosopher, linguist and a poet. He belonged to the sect' Isolationist) (Mon'atezila) author of many ancient poems and proverbs.

7. Ali Ibn Abi Talib(The Imam Ali). Cousin and in son-in-law of the Prophet Mohamed (PBUH) born in Makha, and died in 661. He was known for his legendary courage and wisdom. After his death, some "shia" attributed to him a supernatural power claiming that it was transmitted to him by the Prophet Mohamed (Peace be upon him).

8. Jebran Khalil Jebran, A Lebanese poet and man of letters. Born Lebanon in 1883, he immigrated to the United States where he lived in Boston before going to France to study the beaux-arts. He came back to New York where he started his career. Among his most famous masterpiece is "The Prophet".

9. Alghazali, Abu Hamid born in 1057 in Persia, is one of the most known scholars of Islam; he was a famous leader in sophism. He studied religious sciences and acquired a large Sunnite knowledge .He traveled to Jerusalem, Medina, Damascus and Mekkah. He managed to reconcile between Sharia and sophism, to bring to ascetics a frame highly rational, and to link mysticism to regular Islamic teaching .His glory contributed strongly

to the approval of "Ijmaa" (general consent). He died at the beginning of the 12th century.

10. Almoutanabbi, Abu Taib, born in Kuffa in Iraq, he died in 966. He claimed to be a poet and was one of the most known poets of the Abbassid Era.

11. Abu Nawass, Alhassen Ibn hani, was born in Khouzestan, in the south of Iran in756. He died in 815 and was one the most famous Arab poets of the Abassid era.

12. The Umayyads (661-750).The Umayyads reigned after the Caliphs known as (Rachidin) or martyr. Their first caliph was Maouyia Ibn Abi Soufyian. He transported the capital city of Islam from Medina to Damascus where he was previously a governor. It was an event of great importance. That administration benefited from the help of the Byzantine scribes residing in the area who protected and acquired a notable degree of efficiency and a good ruling. The Caliphs established the administration in Damascus .The Umayyads were the artisans of an immense Islamic expansion. The Muslim armies reached, in the East , the boundaries of China covered in the west, North Africa and Spain and advanced until Poitiers (732).

13. The Abassids (750-1228). It was the end of the 'western Arab kingdom' replaced by a theocratic Asiatic monarchy from Iranian roots. The sovereign who has, by his ascendance, the same Sunnite legitimacy as the Umayyad is first presented as an Imam. The successional system shall be drifted between heirship and election. The dynasty was illustrated by a great sovereign Harun Alrashid, contemporary and correspondent of Charlemagne. It is a period of refined civilization of One Thousand and One Night. But the factor of decadence will soon appear: they devoted themselves to the ostentation of a sumptuous and delicate life. It was the "Vizir", then the Turkish Guard Chief, the admiral Aloumara who in reality held the power.

References

1. Elias Khalil zakhariya Kalila and Dimna - revised and coordinated by, House of Andalus by the Press Edition Beyruth, 1963.

2. La Pajatentra, translation by Dr Abdulhamid Yuness, General Egyptian Authority of the Book, Cairo, 1982.

3. Soresh Koli Speech of the River a masterpiece of the Indian literature translated by Sourial Abdul malik, General Egyptian Authority of the Book, Cairo 1964.

4. Abu Hilal Alaskari Collection of Proverbs revised by Mahmud Abdul FathiIbrahim and Abdul Majid Katymich, Cairo 1964.

5. Cheich Taher Aljazairi, Proverbs the most well known, The House Of Thinking (Darul Fikr) Damascus, Syria, 1920.

6. Rudolf Zilhein, The Ancient Arab Proverbs translated by Dr Ramdan Abdul Tawab, Beirut, 1970.

7. Waddi Albustani, Rubayyat Alkhyiam Beirut, Lebanon 1971.

8. Dr Ramdan Abdoul Tawab, Book of Proverbs of Sadoussi, The House of Arab Awakening, Beirut 1982

9. Hassan Ali Wisdoms and Proverbs, Library of Alexandria, Cairo,1988.

10. Cherif Algalib the Marvelous Flowers Saudi House of Edition and diffusion, 1993.

11. Abderrahmane Alnabloussi, Speech related to Love and Women, House of Wisdom, Darour Lehikhama, Damascus, 1989.

12. Mohamed Kamil Abdossamed, Invitation to a Table of Wisdom New Office University, Alkzandria, Egypt 1991.

13. Almaidany Collection of Proverbs. 1124 J,C The most famous proverbs translated into Latin and printed in Bonn in 1838.

14. Aljahiz, The Animals, Abasside Era revised by Abdousalam Harroun. Beirut, House of the Arab Patrimony Renaissance 3rd edition 1969.

15. Almasoudy, the Gardens of Gold, Edition of Lebanese University, 1975.

16. Alsouba'ai History of Arab Literature, Cairo, Library of the Egyptian Renaissance, 1948.

17. Abdil Majide Abiddine, Proverbs in ancient Arab Poetry, Beirut, 1971.

18. Studies of Easterners Concerning the Authenticity of Pre-Islamic Period (Aljahiliya) Beirut House "Daroul Alime Lilemalayine" House of Science for Million, 1976.

19. Khalid Hassine Saab, Wise Speeches, The Arab Institution of diffusion, Beirut, 1995.

20. Amin Ahmed, Fajrou Islam (The Dawn of Islam) Cairo, 1954.

21. Dr. Riyadh Frayha, The Joke and The Laughter in the Eastern Arab Patrimony of Pre- Islamic Period (Aljahiliya) At the Abasside Era, Modern Library, Beirut,1991.

22. Abdourazakh Abdou Nabih, Speech that Days Cannot Make forgot, Daroul Fikar, Aman, Jordan, 1995.

23. Dr. Mohmoud Tewvikh Abou Ali, Arab Proverbs of Pre- Islamic Period. House of Nakash (Darou Nakash) Beirut, Lebanon, 1988.

24. Jabrane Khalil Jebrane, The Words of Jabran, United House of Edition, Beirut, Lebanon, 1988.

25. Dr. Mahmoude Ghoura, Ears of Time, Nawval Institution, Beirut, Lebanon, 1993.

26. Samir Khane Abdoulah Alsindi, the Kurdish Wisdom, Ministry of Information and Culture, Baghdad, 1979.

27. Pierre Rondot, Islam and Muslim of Today, Edition of Orante, Paris, 1965.

28. Thought and Values of Islam, Unesco, Press, Vol. IV, N I, 1977.

29. La Rousse du XXem Siecle – Paris 1998.

30. Mohtar Katir Joglo, Koranic Wisdom, Enlightened by some Koranic Verses, Paris.Geuthner, 1935

31. Shawqi deif - Period (Aljahiliya) of Pre- Islamic - Cairo, 1999 .

32. Soufan Akef – Values Educatives of Arab proverbs – Ministry of Educatin – Abu Dhabi- U.A.E- 1991.